How to Master Your Monkey Mind

www.penguin.co.uk

How to Master Your Monkey Mind

Overcome anxiety, increase confidence and regain control of your life

Don Macpherson

BANTAM PRESS

TRANSWORLD PUBLISHERS

Penguin Random House, One Embassy Gardens,
8 Viaduct Gardens, London SW11 7BW
www.penguin.co.uk

Transworld is part of the Penguin Random House group of companies
whose addresses can be found at global.penguinrandomhouse.com

First published in Great Britain in 2021 by Bantam Press
an imprint of Transworld Publishers

A CIP catalogue record for this book
is available from the British Library.

ISBN 9781787633575

Text design by Couper Street Type Co.
Typeset in 11.5/16pt Sabon MT Pro by Jouve (UK), Milton Keynes
Printed and bound in Great Britain by Clays Ltd, Elcograf S.p.A.

The authorized representative in the EEA is Penguin Random House Ireland,
Morrison Chambers, 32 Nassau Street, Dublin D02 YH68

Penguin Random House is committed to a sustainable
future for our business, our readers and our planet. This book
is made from Forest Stewardship Council® certified paper.

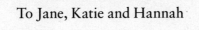

To Jane, Katie and Hannah

'Bring me your brain and I will tune it for you.
Better still, I will explain how you can
service and tune your own brain,
and master your Monkey Mind.'

DON MACPHERSON

Contents

Contents

Contents

10 The Anxiety Buster

Part III: Worrier to Warrior

Introduction

Are you a worrier? Do everyday challenges weigh you down? Do stress and anxiety fog up your mind? Do you wish you could tackle the bigger issues with more confidence and clarity? Do you struggle to stay on track at work, socially, and in life generally? Do you ever really sleep *properly*? How balanced is your relationship with food? Do you look around and see others – maybe friends, colleagues, or even famous individuals – appearing so capable and wonder why that isn't you? Would you like to *stop worrying unnecessarily*?

Your life can change *from this moment*.

I have been studying and working in the field of mind management and mental health for over twenty-five years, and in this book I will draw on that ongoing research and those years of experience to help you tune your own brain and change your life. My approach is a blend of knowledge amassed from working closely and studying with neuroscientists and neurosurgeons; Buddhist teachings; and decades of studying and practising ethical, clinical hypnosis.

Combining these complementary fields of expertise, I have evolved a revolutionary system of Tools that will allow you to take back control of your life. The techniques and ideas in this book have been forensically road-tested during years of mind coaching high-profile clients and members of the public – often in very demanding and, at times, high-risk circumstances. I aim to offer you *actual, real-world Tools* that will teach you how to deal with issues relating to anxiety, sleep, diet, confidence, relationships and more.

You will discover proven and tested techniques to help you:

- understand and change how you breathe in order to help you face down anxiety with confidence and control;
- use language and positivity to Mind the Monkey in your head;
- learn the ancient art of the Kaizen to transform your life, little by little;
- discover the Tool used by Wimbledon-winners to hit that crucial match-winner under the watchful eyes of millions, and learn how this idea can help you visualize and achieve your own goals;
- discover how ideas utilized by a world-leading heart surgeon to remain calm under the life-or-death pressure of the operating theatre can transform your own confidence and performance under stress;

- take a fresh and calmer approach to life, replacing haste and panic with serenity;
- turbo-boost your brain power and self-esteem, strengthening your mental resilience and confidence;
- use the power of your brain to boost your immune system;
- and sleep properly, waking up feeling refreshed, positive and raring to go!

I will explain the concept of the so-called Monkey Mind, which I have been working with ever since I first read about its origins over twenty years ago. Since then I have absorbed the notion into my daily working practice, complementing it with a comprehensive knowledge of modern neuroscience. By definition, these are deeply complex and challenging academic subjects whose complexity is often simply too difficult for many individuals to grasp (particularly people with pre-existing mental challenges). It has been my long-standing ambition to take these topics and make them *accessible and understandable to a wider audience.*

My unique package of Tools will equip you with techniques to bounce back from adversity and struggles – real or perceived – using mental training that has been tried and tested by international sports stars, celebrities, and hundreds of everyday people. Success on the outside begins with success on the inside, and this book will show you how to learn and master my Tools so that you will be able to take charge of your own life and become your own mind coach.

Each Tool is illustrated with a case study from a real-world situation, to demonstrate how these techniques have transformed lives.

In the past I have started to read so many books on the subject of mind management, and – to be perfectly honest – I have put them down halfway through. I was looking for advice and help, and I found myself blinded by science. I don't want you to find yourself in a similar position – so let me do the heavy lifting for you, by taking elements of ancient teachings, hypnosis, neuroscience and modern mind management in order to give you the Tools to take control of your mind. Whatever the scale of your challenge, and no matter how entrenched your issues, this book will equip you with the Tools and knowledge to *permanently transform* yourself from Worrier to Warrior.

Part I

The Monkey Whisperer

The Monkey Whisperer's Story

I guess if I'm going to be poking around inside your head, I should at least introduce myself properly. It would be rude not to. So let me explain briefly the journey that has brought me to the most rewarding job in the world.

Some say your school days are the best years of your life, but I've never really understood why anyone would think that – mine certainly weren't. Far from it, in fact. I just couldn't, or wouldn't, apply myself at school. Exam time was always horrendously stressful, although that might have had something to do with the fact I never bothered to do the necessary revision! To make matters worse, my parents were both very successful, hard-working, popular, and doing everything they could to ensure I had a good education – and there I was, seemingly wasting that opportunity.

My mum was a very clever lady from Derbyshire who became a grammar-school teacher and then went on to be a Justice of the Peace. My dad was an old-fashioned, old-school doctor, in the sense that he had time for everybody. In the 1960s, he was brave enough to leave a comfortable practice where he was about to become the senior doctor to instead take up a role as the local GP in a so-called overspill estate called Hattersley on the outskirts of Manchester.

At that time they were knocking down the city's slums and building tall blocks of flats. Hattersley turned out to be one of the most economically challenged estates of all, yet my dad stayed in a flat there because it was too far from home to commute on a daily basis. He was the only doctor for about two thousand people, all of whom were struggling to make ends meet in this very deprived area. He worked incredibly hard – always trying to do more for his patients, always going the extra mile, always trying to better himself.

Even though I was relatively young, I was full of admiration for this man who gave up a soft number for something as challenging as that. Many years later, I was especially touched when my dad's funeral cortège passed through Hattersley on its way to the church and the streets were lined with people applauding. That really resonated with me. Seeing this reaction from people he had tried to help made a big impact on me that day. Even though he wasn't there to see it, that was his ultimate reward.

I was born in 1949 into a post-war ration period of austerity. When I was growing up, all the adults around me had been through the war. Most, if not all, had lost someone or, at the very least, had been severely impacted on a personal level by those years. So, as a young lad, whenever anything was bothering me, people would just say, 'What have you got to worry about? You don't need to wonder whether your house will still be standing in the morning or whether your father might not come home from battle.'

There wasn't a great deal of time for any kids with anxieties or worries. Society was a bit fed up and, indeed, a bit beaten up. 'Intolerant' is an excellent word to describe most people's attitude to youth back then.

By contrast, my parents made sure I treated everybody with respect, whether they were dustbin men or multi-millionaires. I watched them both around the community and it was clear my parents were 'people's people'. I would say they were very 'Northern', at least in terms of their ethics – they treated everyone the same, and would chat to anyone they met. Inevitably, that had a heavy influence on my own world view.

I scraped through the entrance exam for Stockport Grammar School, but during my teens I found education a real battle. I was rubbish in class. I just didn't get it. I had a bit of a rebellious streak in me, which didn't help. Not sure where that came from, as both my parents were very stoic, but nonetheless, it did get me in some bother occasionally. For example, I refused to wear the school cap, and I think I probably still own the world record for most detentions as a result! At other times I would imitate the teachers' voices to make my mates laugh. Nothing really serious, I was just a bit of a clown. My reports started off with the classic 'could do better'. Then, as the teachers' patience started to wane over the years, the comments turned into 'must do better'. By the time I was in the final year, I think it was all they could do not to write 'lazy little s**t'!

I failed nearly all of my exams and felt as if I had let my parents down. By then, the school had given up on me, to be honest. However, my predictably poor exam results allowed – or maybe forced – me to follow a more entrepreneurial route, to be more creative. But how? I had absolutely no idea where I was going, or what I wanted 'to be'.

Luckily for me, various big companies used to work with local schools, finding kids who were never going to go on to further education but who could work as apprentices. One day, I was summoned to the headmaster's office with no warning, where this guy from Mobil Oil chatted to me. Fortunately, he liked me and offered me a placement. So that was it, my get-away route, escape from Colditz through the front door, no need to dig tunnels. I couldn't believe my luck. To paraphrase Tolkien, 'All who wander are not lost!'

The job was filing papers, in the pre-computer days of April 1967, and I was paid around £700 a year. I'd get the train into work and loved it from the very first minute. For a start, I wasn't at school – that was a huge bonus. But also, rationing had become a thing of the past, I was seventeen, had a job and a car, and my life had just taken off in terms of fun. Manchester was really buzzing in the sixties: United ruled the world of football, there were always famous bands in town and celebrities hanging out in the clubs, the city was alive with all sorts of interesting people. It was just a great place to be.

Every time I hear Procol Harum's 'A Whiter Shade Of Pale' I can see myself as a young lad, walking down Deansgate in a blue suit, white shirt and black shoes, on my way to work for Mobil Oil. I'd escaped school and I was free, stopping off at the Magnet Café – which was so greasy that you couldn't see through the windows – to order eggs, chips and beans every day.

I worked hard as a filing clerk, got promoted and, before I knew it, somebody else was filing away my paperwork. Even so, I wasn't satisfied. After about a year of that I wanted more – I was always hungry for knowledge. The next step was working as a sales rep, on the road with a car. Before long, a position came up at Dunlop and I made the leap to that big company, which had a large sales depot based in Ardwick, on the outskirts of the city centre. I was still selling over the phone, but there was a clear career progression so I felt very motivated.

After a few months in Ardwick I was transferred to Bath, where I have lived ever since (forty-seven years at the time of writing). I warmed to the West Country people – they seemed to quite like my Northern accent and I quite liked their laid-back attitude – and the air seemed a bit clearer, even though the beer was warm and flat.

I'd been promoted to the role of salesman on the road, which is what I'd wanted, so I couldn't say no. At just twenty-two, I was the youngest salesman in the company. I stayed with Dunlop for about fifteen years. However, although the job was well paid and my colleagues were mostly nice people, I started to want out – I never felt as if I fully blended in to the corporate world. So, in my late twenties I started to look around for a way out. During this time, I took a hiatus from working at Dunlop and had spells in a sports shop. I even tried to get a job as a presenter on the local TV channel. They offered me the job but it would have meant moving from Bath, which I didn't want to do, so my telly career was over before it had even begun!

At the age of thirty-three, I finally left Dunlop, and in 1983 I started my own business as a marketing consultant, travelling to various tyre companies and asking them if they needed my help to develop their business. Most of my work was largely results-driven, so suddenly there was no guarantee I'd be able to pay my mortgage or even put food on the table. However, that lack of security keeps you hungry. If you wake up in the morning and don't know how you are going to pay your bills, you get up even though you might be tired and stressed. You're focused on getting results, because you have to.

For the first six years it was hard graft, hand to mouth, juggling lots of small contracts and clients just to pay the bills. At times I simply wasn't earning enough. Meanwhile, I'd started playing tennis and, by coincidence, one of the people I played against – and soon became friends with – was the musician Peter Gabriel. One day, I asked Peter if he could use my services developing his recording studio business, and although he politely declined, he did say he knew a Japanese entrepreneur called Hiroshi Kato who might really benefit from what I did. This chap was involved with the Brabham motor-racing family, so I was really interested to meet him.

Long story short, through Hiroshi Kato I met and became very good friends with the motorsport legend and three-times Formula One world champion, Sir Jack Brabham OBE. Over the coming months we got to know each other quite well. Then, at a glitzy motorsports awards ceremony in December 1989, Sir Jack asked if I would help him to look after his son, David, who was a very promising racing driver. Referencing my lengthy experience in sponsorship, sales and marketing, Sir Jack felt I was well-equipped to help David navigate the demanding financial and political pitfalls of a career in high-level motorsport.

How could I refuse? My life changed from that moment.

Four years later and I am with David Brabham at Imola for the San Marino F1 Grand Prix. He is driving for the fledgling Simtek team, owned by the young and talented Nick Wirth. It is David's second year in F1 – the first season in 1990 was, to say the least, a steep learning curve. The curve was about to get even steeper . . .

It is Saturday, 30 April 1994, and the qualifying session for the San Marino Grand Prix is about twenty minutes old. Back in those days, F1 cars were very fast and made a wonderful noise that you could almost feel through your body from the side of the track. I am watching from the corner where Rubens Barrichello had a particularly nasty crash in practice the day before, a chilling precursor to the horrors that are about to unfold.

Suddenly, things go quiet, very quiet. It can mean only one thing – there must have been an accident, and the continuing silence suggests it is likely to have been a bad one.

After what feels like an eternity, the cars come towards me slowly. Anxiously, I strain to look for David's car, and am mightily relieved when he comes into view, but where is David's teammate, Roland Ratzenberger? I had chatted to him and wished him good luck less than an hour ago. Earlier that morning we exchanged banter at the hotel as he climbed into his Porsche and headed for the circuit. He was a lovely guy with a great sense of humour, and a fine, brave driver who at long last was living his dream racing in Formula One.

Roland's car never came into view, no matter how much I willed it to. On track, his car had sustained slight damage to the front wing, which flew off at an incredibly high speed. From that moment Roland was just a passenger in his vehicle as it smashed into a concrete wall at 180 mph, resulting in what proved to be fatal injuries.

Back at the hotel – without Roland – I remember David asking me if I thought he should race the next day. I replied in the only way I could at that time. 'Only you can decide,' I said. David did race, as much to raise the spirit and morale of the emotionally shattered Simtek mechanics as anything else, and to this day I don't think he has received full credit for his very brave and selfless decision. David would later say, 'I thought, *I have to pick this team up and continue what we are doing*, so I decided to race, really, for the guys.'

Unfortunately, that harrowing experience was not the end of this particular horror story. The next day, during the grand prix itself, the F1 legend Ayrton Senna crashed and was killed. The entire world of motorsport fell into mourning. Everyone was in shock. Two drivers dead in two days.

That weekend was the point at which I realized I was not doing enough for David, and that I should find out as much as possible about the huge mental stresses associated with Formula One. Not just on the drivers, but on the team personnel too. No one seemed to know how to deal with the shock of losing Roland and Ayrton. Many tears were shed privately, behind closed doors. But who could they talk to? I guess back then they just went home and dealt with it as best they could . . . Yet these people – hundreds of people involved with the whole F1 circus at the circuit, thousands more around the world – had only a few days to recover before they were back at work for the next race, the Monaco Grand Prix.

I was overwhelmed by the wish that I could have been able to help David and the Simtek F1 team far more in coming to terms with Roland's death, but back in 1994, I didn't know what I didn't know. This communally traumatic weekend had a severe impact on everyone who experienced it; for me, I was suddenly asking questions about myself, my purpose, my path in life.

I was walking around the pits looking at the young racers, some clearly in shock. There we were, surrounded by these cars where every part of their design is the pinnacle of engineering, where optimum performance is embedded into every nut and bolt, yet the attention paid to the mental well-being of the drivers in this incredibly dangerous sport was decades behind.

I quickly became a man on a mission. I started to study mind management intensely, obsessively. I read hundreds of books, from clinical neuroscience to self-help. Having hardly read a book at school, I became an insatiable reader, poring over book after book about the human brain. I delved into titles on psychology, neuroscience, psychiatry, neurology . . . I didn't care how diverse they were, I wanted everyone's opinion on how the brain works.

Even more crucially, I realized I was privileged to be around the F1 pit lane and therefore blessed with first-hand access to the individuals who were dealing with this terrible loss most closely – the racers themselves. Yes, team personnel felt the tragedy, of course they did, but it was the drivers who were being asked to go back out on the tracks in the same cars, even though so much uncertainty still remained about the causes of these fatal incidents.

How would these young racing drivers deal with that? How would it affect their driving? Who would cope with it best, and why? What lasting effect might it have on their wellbeing? What systems were in place to help them?

I had to learn more so that I could help. I was able to ask

several racers directly how they dealt with the stress, the travelling, the dangers, and how they bounced back when things didn't go to plan. The warriors of the Formula One inner circle were especially helpful to me, and to this day I feel particularly lucky to have had the opportunity to learn so much from them.

My journey from manager to mind coach had begun . . . I had 'reversed' into mind coaching and, in so doing, discovered what has since become my life's obsession.

Around the start of the millennium I was working with a particular Formula One racing driver and had formed a really good relationship with him. This hadn't been difficult as he was great fun to be with, and a very talented driver. In reality, I was probably learning more from him than he was from me!

However, it turned out that things weren't going quite as well as I thought, because one day he told me he was getting a little tired of the 'talkie bits' – our one-to-one sessions. He reckoned he had fully got my 'message' that he needed to be more calm, relaxed and confident, but wondered when I was actually going to show him 'how to'. He was, quite rightly, looking to me for some mental Tools that he could take into battle, *Tools that would actually work* when he most needed to be calm, relaxed and confident.

This was a big wake-up call for me. I'd thought I was doing a reasonably good job as his mind coach, but he was absolutely correct. I realized I needed to up my game and do more for these brave drivers. Encouraged by this racer's feedback and that of other clients, I began to assemble my own Tool Box of practical techniques and ideas.

Some Tools were more obvious than others, such as slowing down your breathing to be calmer. But what about Tools to tune confidence, or to concentrate for longer, and more deeply and productively? Or to slow down both your thinking and your life? Or to tackle the biggest problem that repeatedly presents itself with my clients – anxiety?

Over the next few years, I refined, added and expanded these Tools until I had produced what I felt was an invaluable resource for anyone wanting to manage their so-called Monkey Mind. What I had was a menu of mental Tools created through listening to feedback from a long list of world-class sportspeople, high-profile individuals, and others who were successful in a multitude of areas. It was a Tool Box forged in the heat of battle, if you will, where it really mattered most.

What Is the Monkey Mind?

Even though I am truly fascinated by the brain, it's hard not to argue that modern neuroscience leaves plenty of room for confusion. Over the years I have waded through some pretty tall piles of fairly laborious books and texts, and have come to understand fully some bewildering terms in the field, such as 'hippocampus' and 'amygdala'. For example, I now know that the hippocampus is in fact a big cheese when it comes to your emotions, and it also plays a vital role in your brain in your memory and knowledge. The amygdala is essentially the chief executive of your emotions and, in fact, your behaviour in general. It can be pretty intimidating to read about all this terminology, particularly when you consider that some readers might be coming to books with pre-existing mental challenges. I prefer to explain these complex principles and processes as simply as possible.

I would like to think I am in good company. Take the famous smart-arse Albert Einstein – whose brain, somewhat ironically, turned out to be smaller than average when scientists had a poke inside (after he died, I presume). Now, before you tut at me, I'm not comparing myself to Einstein, but he and I do have one thing in common . . . We both love simplicity. In fact, the patents-clerk-turned-universe-changing-genius once said, 'Everything should be made as simple as possible, but not simpler.'

Figuring that Einstein knew a fair bit about such things, let's simplify the answer to the most common questions I get asked: What is the Monkey Mind? Who is the Monkey? Where does it live? What does it do?

During my extensive research into how the brain works, I stumbled upon the idea in Buddhist teachings that everyone has a Monkey in their head, chattering, over-reacting, crashing about, screeching for attention and causing mental anguish. This Buddhist idea is the origin of the theory of the Monkey Mind, said to resemble a restless monkey in a jungle, swinging from tree to tree, aimlessly (and often unhelpfully) commentating on anything and everything. Your Monkey is prattling away in your head constantly, advising and directing you, rather like the satnav in your car. It has two main jobs above all other duties: to keep you safe and attempt to stop you making a fool of yourself. Unless suitably tamed, this Monkey is capable of causing catastrophic and highly toxic damage to an individual's wellbeing – it can fuel anxiety, restlessness, confusion and fear. Learning to 'tame' your Monkey and stop it from wreaking havoc is therefore pivotal to leading a happy and fulfilling life.

Multiple triggers can set the Monkey off on a crash course

for causing trouble, such as ongoing stresses, worries or situations causing anxiety in a person's life. The problem is that uncontrolled Monkey chatter can create a cycle of behaviour that spirals and deteriorates very quickly.

Modern neuroscience has now caught up with – and endorsed – these age-old theories. When the Monkey is crashing about, causing all these problems, a very specific neuroscientific process is occurring in the brain. Essentially, the Monkey causes a chemical imbalance.

Most people have heard of how endorphins are released during and after physical exercise, and how the release of the 'happy chemical', serotonin, is triggered by pleasant events or thoughts. Then there's oxytocin, the 'cuddle chemical', and, of course, dopamine, known as the 'reward chemical'. When the Monkey is stressed and begins careering around inside the brain, the culprit is adrenalin. You could say that the Monkey is Chief Executive of Adrenalin Production, regardless of how much is required (if any). It is looking for a fire to put out, searching for an impending emergency, when in reality there almost never is one.

Unfortunately, once triggered, this powerful chemical reaction can play havoc with the mind and the nervous system. Simply telling someone to 'calm down' or 'not to worry' won't work, because there is a clear pattern of chemical activity already happening in this adrenalin-soaked brain that cannot be switched off easily. If the Monkey remains unmanaged and is unwittingly allowed to keep the adrenalin on full chat, a person will very quickly feel increasingly anxious. This can lead to spiralling difficulties and, ultimately, to significant mental health issues unless the situation is resolved . . . But how?

Well, the brain has two hemispheres – left and right – like two halves of a walnut. The left hemisphere is concerned with logic, and this is where the Monkey lives, in charge of your language skills, as well as your analysing, judging, planning and processing capabilities. In more simple terms, the Monkey could be called your conscious mind, and it is on duty all day until it eventually falls asleep.

At this point, the Night Porter takes over. This is your subconscious mind, predominantly the right hemisphere of your brain, where you do things instinctively, without thinking. The subconscious mind sees 'the bigger picture' of your life, is more subtle, non-verbal, and goes by gut feelings, using all your senses.

Of course, the subconscious mind never rests. During the daytime it works closely and effectively (if all is well) with the conscious Monkey Mind. It is only at night, when the Monkey 'crashes out', that the subconscious is working solo. This Night Porter then makes sure everything continues to function – your heart beats, your lungs function, your blood flows – and allows the natural stages of sleep to occur, such as dreaming, until the conscious mind – your Monkey – wakes up about seven hours later, and resumes duties as a new day dawns.

Ideally, during the daytime, the two halves of the brain should work together harmoniously, automatically, and when they do, you experience the wonderful feeling of being balanced, grounded and centred; you feel safe and in control, which is what all humans really need to live a happy, healthy, fulfilled life, and to maximize our potential.

However, when either one of these halves is too dominant (especially the left hemisphere), or maybe even just temporarily 'out of order', things can turn to custard very quickly. In the case of the Monkey, problems arise when it attempts to dominate the brain from its 'house' in the left hemisphere. This can sometimes overwhelm the right hemisphere, often at totally inappropriate times, like some big, hairy, uninvited guest crashing a party at precisely the wrong moment . . . But the Monkey can't help itself – it loves to meddle, constantly commentating and advising on everything and anything you are doing or about to do.

You might be wondering what would happen if we didn't have a Monkey Mind? Good question. The fact is, *if you did not have a Monkey Mind at all, and if the Monkey Mind had malfunctioned completely*, then I'm afraid you would be in a spot of bother for altogether different reasons.

Prolonged stress or worry – such as when an ongoing unresolved situation is creating extreme anxiety – can cause the Monkey Mind to malfunction as it continues to attempt to find solutions. This leads to the two halves of the brain becoming chronically imbalanced, which can leave you vulnerable to more serious issues, such as depression – but don't worry, there is plenty you can do before you ever reach that stage.

Remember, we all need a conscious Monkey Mind to keep us safe, to be our filter in life, and to plan ... but have you ever wondered what would happen if something catastrophic happened to the left side of your brain, where the Monkey lives, and suddenly you did not have a Monkey Mind at all?

A completely 'Out of Order' (closed until further notice), non-existent Monkey Mind might cause some or all of the below:

- No memories, long- or short-term
- A feeling of being detached from normality
- No ego
- Total silence in your head
- No likes or dislikes
- Poor relationships, problems relating to people
- No order, no planning, no structure to your life
- No worries, no stress, no inhibitions
- No fear
- No phobias (even if you had any, you wouldn't be aware of them)
- Thinking only in pictures – not words – but without any colour
- Just 'being', hanging out in the beauty of the universe
- Experiencing life as one big Glastonbury Festival

Some of the above might sound pretty cool, huh? BUT – and this is a bigger 'but' than any previous 'but' – you would not be safe, you would be totally unable to recognize danger, and would be completely blind to risk. You wouldn't perceive the idea of jogging in the wrong direction along the fast lane of the M4 as remotely risky.

By way of illustrating this concept with a specific story, let me tell you about one of the most remarkable brain scientists who has ever blessed us with their expertise: the neuroanatomist Jill Bolte Taylor. Jill was just thirty-seven years old when a blood vessel burst in her brain and she suffered a stroke. Observing her own condition through the eyes of a world expert – effectively witnessing her own brain shutting down – Jill was somehow able to chronicle her disintegration into being unable to walk, talk, read or write, as well as the chronic memory loss she suffered.

Jill was experiencing in real time what happens when your Monkey Mind totally malfunctions and falls completely silent – she had no voice in her head, no Monkey chatter. Only the right hemisphere of her brain was working and she felt peaceful, loving, joyful and compassionate. But – and this is another big 'but' – it meant there was nobody at home in the left side of her brain. The co-pilot's seat was empty, there was no planning or instruction, no one advising, analysing or generally looking after her. In fact, she was no longer safe . . .

Jill recorded the process in her amazing book, *My Stroke of Insight* (with her mother), gifting us a truly unique insight into how the brain works under extreme physical duress. I came across her book during my research on the malfunctioning of the brain and I realized that what she was talking about dovetailed with the ideas I was teaching – for me, this book remains a genuinely inspirational and highly influential piece of work. Jill sheds light on the relationship between the left and right sides of our brain in a way that no one else has ever done. I urge you to read it; Jill is an inspirational woman who, incredibly, has recovered so well that she continues to study, teach and practise to this day.

Jill's extreme experience illustrates perfectly why we all need to appreciate our Monkey Mind – it has a valid role to play in keeping us safe – but it needs to be tamed and controlled. Your Monkey cannot be allowed to rampage unhindered through your life. If you don't make any effort to manage your Monkey Mind, it will take full advantage of your *laissez-faire* attitude and run your life for you . . . and then there's the potential for things to become very chaotic indeed. You hear the term 'mind management' thrown around a lot in sport and life coaching, but what I really want to say here is Mind the Monkey!

Hopefully, you will now see why it is important for you to understand at least a little of the neuroscience at work here – in order to check whether your brain's two halves are in sync and, more importantly, if they aren't, how you can retune them to a more harmonious state so that hopefully normal service can be resumed.

I have been studying and using the concept of the Monkey Mind in my practice for over twenty years. Some people even call me the Monkey Whisperer. The nickname was first used by a client who, on listening to the personal mp3 (a twenty-minute audio recording I make for my clients, which reflects the essence of our one-to-one private session) that I had recorded for her, said the calm and whispered reassurances reminded her of her father reading a bedtime story. The name seems to have stuck.

Well, now it is your turn to benefit. I am here to help you become calm, relaxed and confident . . . So let's press on and start taking control of that Monkey.

Part II

The Tools

Tool 1

Zen Breathing

How to Be Calm and Relaxed

Of all the mental Tools I have used in over twenty-five years of work, the one that has produced the best feedback from clients by far is called Zen Breathing. I must admit to being surprised that this is overwhelmingly the case, but considering that even the marathon runners I work with have forgotten how to breathe effectively, maybe I shouldn't be so shocked after all. Even the word 'respiration' is derived from the Latin *'spirare'*, meaning 'to breathe', and 'spirit' and 'inspire' are both directly linked to this root too.

Incredibly, most people don't know how to breathe well! They do so in a very shallow way – sometimes referred to as 'upside-down breathing' – meaning they breathe only, or mainly, from their chest. It seems that we become 'upside-down breathers' at a young age – possibly around seven or eight. You can see children younger than that breathe in a wonderfully relaxed way, albeit completely subconsciously, of course. Whether this change in breathing is related to children becoming more aware of the world around them, peer pressure, ever greater demands put on them at school, increased social awareness (and therefore a subsequent increase in the role of the Monkey Mind in their young lives), and so on, is open to discussion. But after that age, it is quite common to see children taking short, shallow breaths. Adults are certainly affected by this ineffective breathing habit, too. To be honest, I myself was an 'upside-down breather' until I began to study breathing techniques and the effects such inefficient techniques have on the body and mind!

There is a self-perpetuating situation at work here: if your breath is shallow, you are more likely to become anxious; unfortunately, when you are anxious, your breath is more likely to become, or remain, shallow. When we are anxious or stressed, our breath is one of the first functions that we lose control of. Our heart rate increases, our pulse quickens, our chest tightens, we might feel hotter – all of which means we struggle to breathe properly and it becomes difficult to regain control of our Monkey Mind. Anxiety seems to 'jam' the diaphragm and we become 'upside-down breathers'. The shallow breaths we take mean our lungs do not fill fully with oxygen, which can lead to feeling short of breath, which in turn fuels feelings of anxiety.

I began to research the science behind this issue, and the more I studied the more I realized that inefficient breathing can be a blight on most people's everyday lives. I became determined to do something about my own breathing and, as I made progress, I was shocked by the improvements . . .

I coined the term Zen Breathing to describe what is often known as 'diaphragmatic breathing'. It's a concept that first started to emerge in academic circles during the 1970s, and its benefits are now long established. From a personal point of view, I discovered Zen Breathing quickly reduced my anxiety while greatly improving my ability to maintain perspective on life's challenges. Remember this: on average, we inhale and exhale twenty-five thousand times per day. For something we do so often to be out of control – or, at best, not to be calm and considered – seems like a recipe for problems.

The great news about Zen Breathing is that this super-beneficial technique is already at our fingertips. We all have the power to do it, no matter how ingrained we think our problems or challenges are.

So, what exactly is Zen Breathing, and why is it so effective in terms of controlling anxiety and maintaining good mental health? Simply put, Zen Breathing is taking back control of our inhalations and exhalations – *consciously* taking control.

Find yourself a quiet space for a few moments, somewhere that you can work on your Zen Breathing without being interrupted. Lie down on the floor (gravity helps you connect to the rhythm of your breath) and put one hand on your tummy/abs and the other hand on your chest to check you are engaging your diaphragm. As you gently breathe in and out, the hand that moves up or down the most must be the one on your tummy. If you find the hand on your chest is moving up and down, then your breathing is too shallow – not a problem, it's good that you have found that out. Instead, focus on breathing using your diaphragm, as I have explained, until your tummy moves up and down, rather than your upper chest.

Next, we need to introduce a counting procedure. As I breathe in slowly through my nose, I count to three, then I hold the breath for a couple of seconds or so, before releasing it (through my nose or mouth, whichever is most comfortable) to a count of five, six, seven, eight or nine. The pause after the in-breath is like the moment before a golfer's swing when they make sure they are set correctly and generate a sense of control.

The trick is to *make the out-breath longer than the in-breath.* We do this because your heartbeat actually speeds up slightly when you breathe in, but when you breathe out your heartbeat slows down, so taking a longer out-breath maximizes this beneficial physical effect. It's up to you what counting procedure you choose, but in my opinion (and based on considerable feedback from clients), it's essential to make sure those out-breaths are longer than the in-breaths. The longer out-breath is also necessary because the full intake of replenishing oxygen is matched by carbon dioxide being fully exhaled from the body. All of this elicits the relaxation response and generates a sense of calm and control.

Have a go at breathing this way for a short while, until

you find a relaxed rhythm and only the hand on your tummy is rising and falling. Now, close your eyes and simply connect to the gentle rhythm of your Zen Breaths while telling your breath to *slow down, slow down, slow . . . down.* Keeping your eyes closed, picture your hand on your tummy moving gently up as you breathe in, and down as you breathe out (of course, you can also feel it moving, too).

Essentially, if you stay with your Zen Breathing for as long as you can, and remain focused, you will be meditating. Meditation is exactly the same as concentration, which is the boss of *all* mental skills (we will come to how Zen Breathing can benefit your powers of concentration later in this book, see Tool 5 – page 107).

A word of caution: the chances are that, when you first use this Tool, you will hear your Monkey Mind piping up, 'This is boring, you need to check your emails . . . Have you sent that text? When are you taking the dog for a walk? What about getting the car fixed?' This is perfectly normal. The trick is to calmly recognize that you have become distracted. The moment you realize you are not in the now is the very moment you are back in the now – and the sooner you become aware of that, the sooner you can get back to enjoying the benefits of your relaxed breathing.

It's very important not to worry if you do get distracted, because this will only undermine your calm. It simply isn't the case that if your rhythm is broken then your efforts have been ruined. All you need to do is stay relaxed, gently return to your Zen Breathing and carry on.

Ideally, if you can practise Zen Breathing once or twice a day, just for a few minutes at a time, it will soon prove extremely helpful. Like everything, practice will enable you to improve and then, when you need the help of this Tool, you will be able to switch it on easily and effectively.

When you are fully engaged with your Zen Breathing, what exactly is happening in your body? The Zen Breathing is relaxing your mind but also literally flooding your body with loads of oxygen. Your lungs are working as efficiently as possible and your body is receiving the optimum amount of freshly oxygenated blood it requires. The air will flood in through your nose and into your lungs. Your heartbeat will gradually slow down, your blood pressure will lower, and you can now encourage richly oxygenated blood to any part of your body that might need some extra care and attention.

By relaxing the diaphragm with the longer out-breath, Zen Breathing stimulates what is known as the parasympathetic nervous system, and by doing so it reduces the impact of the sympathetic nervous system, which is where your Monkey lives. It also breaks the vicious cycle of adrenalin surging round your body, therefore reducing anxiety and cutting panic attacks off at the pass.

If you are over-thinking things and feeling anxious, you have let your Monkey Mind take over or, at the very least, interfere with the clarity of your thoughts. Zen Breathing can put the Monkey back in its place and quieten the mind. If your Monkey is shouting louder and louder, pouring petrol on to the fire, then switching on your Zen Breathing will stop that happening and re-introduce a lovely sense of calm.

Zen Breathing offers a safe little island for you to make sense of what's bothering the Monkey; it is a place of sanctuary. Your Monkey might be demanding answers and action, but all you need is a little time to re-assert control. Being in control of your breath helps you feel in control of your thoughts and emotions. Every time you connect consciously to your breath you are fully 'here, now', totally living your life in the present and not being dragged back into the past, or into the 'what ifs' of the future.

By concentrating on your breathing, you are making sure you are focused on the present moment. Your breath is always 'here, now' – it can't be anywhere else! With that focus comes clarity on what matters in your life, what you are aiming to achieve and in so doing, Zen Breathing will give you a laser-like focus on your challenges.

If you are really struggling to focus on your breathing and find yourself drifting off into thoughts and scenarios that start to make you feel anxious or overwhelmed again, then one tip to concentrate your efforts is to hum as you breathe out. Believe it or not, it is actually very difficult to think at the same time as you hum, and the sound itself also tells your brain and body that you are relaxed. Some sportspeople often whistle or hum when they feel under stress, and it can help with your Zen Breathing, too.

You will soon get into the habit of switching on your Zen Breathing easily and quickly. Conscious breathing brings together your mind and body, which will help you to feel centred, grounded and balanced, and to create a wonderful feeling of being in control of your emotions, your thoughts (the Monkey Mind) and your body's motor skills.

As you learn to master the art of breathing from your diaphragm, you will soon notice that, more often than not, Zen Breathing will do the trick and quickly begin to calm you down. However, if you are faced with a challenge that really tests you and you find that your breathing is still more shallow than you would ideally like, then I have a 'top-up' technique, which you can keep up your sleeve for those particularly demanding moments: my Three Deeper Breaths. It is simple and super-effective . . .

On the first out-breath, say to yourself silently, 'I am calm'; on the second out-breath say, 'And I am relaxed' to yourself; and on the third out-breath, it's, 'And I am confident'. By using these words, known as mantras (there's more on mantras in Tool 2: Mind the Monkey! – page 51), you are adding even more power to your Zen Breathing Tool. When you are mentally calm and physically relaxed, these two states of being work in tandem so that you automatically feel more confident, which will quickly reduce any anxiety to a much more appropriate level.

Bring the mantra together with – or if you prefer, without – the Zen Breathing, and say to yourself (or out loud), 'I am calm, relaxed and confident', allowing you to feel and be more competent, whatever challenge you are facing.

*

Now that you know what Zen Breathing is and how to use this vital Tool, *when* should you switch it on? There are two main types of situation in your day-to-day life when this will be your go-to Tool: proactive and reactive.

The first is a form of preparation: specific examples might be before a big meeting, a presentation or speech; the sportspeople I work with use it before a race, ahead of a big match and even during games. A golfer I work with has told me he's used it during high-pressure putts in the Ryder Cup. There's even a racing driver who uses it during the warm-up lap of a grand prix. For sportspeople, calmer breathing means their body is fully fuelled, but for the everyday person, Zen Breathing will yield similarly positive benefits ahead of many particular challenges.

Secondly, Zen Breathing is brilliant as a reactive Tool. In the same way that elite athletes use it, Zen Breathing is your go-to Tool the very moment you become aware that you are beginning to feel inappropriately anxious about something, or a little worried or challenged. Maybe you have been on the receiving end of some bad exam results, or an unexpected bill, or an unsolicited phone call that has caused stress. When this happens and catches you by surprise, the first thing I would do (if possible) is sit down (which you might want to do anyway because you'll probably be feeling physically weak), keep your body as still as you can, shut your eyes if it's safe to do so, and switch on the Zen Breathing – then just stay with that as long as you can. In the first few moments it will be tough, because the

Monkey will be screaming at you, 'This is really bad!' but you have got to buy yourself some time.

It will be challenging to start with . . . You might not even feel the benefits, but they will be there: the breathing will be lowering your blood pressure and taking the edge off your over-revving engine, so stick with it and reinforce the habit. Keep practising, because there are a multitude of moments when this particular Tool will be your single biggest ally.

This breathing technique is not just an idea – it is backed up by neuroscience. Eminent brain scientists such as Jill Bolte Taylor suggest that it takes approximately ninety seconds for a negative thought (or any thought) to pass right through your body/system, no matter how ugly/strong/packed with emotion that thought is. Thoughts attached to emotion are *always* stronger – especially negative ones or memories – so you can follow the logic that if you can switch on your Zen Breathing for those ninety seconds, the immediate hit of adrenalin and other stress-causing chemicals will start to dissipate.

Crucially, Zen Breathing is also the most portable of all the mental Tools in this book because, of course, it's something you take with you everywhere you go. This can prove particularly useful because Zen Breathing can help with situations other than the obvious stresses or anxiety-inducing ones. For example, what if you are hoping to lose weight – or, at least, be more careful with your diet? You can use Zen Breathing to help proactively, such as when you go to the supermarket. Doing a few minutes of Zen Breathing before you get out of the car will lower your heart rate and blood pressure, and introduce an immediate sense of calm. Then, when you walk through the doors and are invariably met by the smell of the bakery, or maybe the sight of mountains of sweets and chocolate by the tills, you will already have a measured feeling of control. Zen breathing will help you calm down the adrenalin surging around your Monkey Mind and allow you to make the right decisions.

Zen Breathing is also one of my very favourite Tools because it is discreet – you can breathe consciously without anyone else noticing. You can do it on a bus, on the Tube, queueing at the shops . . . You can even do it when waiting to board a plane. In fact, almost anywhere, any time. No one will even know!

I know Zen Breathing can provide dramatic results because I have been using it with my clients, including elite athletes and sportspeople, for years, and the outcome is always incredible. You would think that high-performance athletes would already be in tune with their bodies – and to some degree you'd be right. However, I've lost count of the number of times a sportsperson has come to me for a session – a perfect physical specimen who has spent years honing and training their physique – and when I check how they are breathing, I can *see* they are doing so incorrectly – all in the upper chest, like a sergeant major.

Another example of the enormous benefits Zen Breathing

can bring came during an intense spell working with a number of young racing drivers at a motorsport team academy. As part of my analysis, I hooked up the drivers to what are known as heart variability monitors (HVMs). This equipment records not only the beats per minute (BPM), but also the *amount of time* that elapses between each beat – which translates to the quality of their breathing.

I used Zen Breathing in conjunction with these machines and we were able to quantify precise benefits very quickly – as the racer improved his breathing technique, we saw a greater consistency in the regularity of his heart rate; his clarity of decision-making improved; and, inevitably, his lap times improved.

Racing drivers love data: they want lap times, cornering speeds, tyre pressures, G-forces. They consume it hungrily and use that knowledge to achieve faster times. When we were able to show these racing drivers a graph on the HVM illustrating how Zen Breathing was making them feel much calmer and more focused, their reactions were priceless. If this Tool can do that for some of the best racing drivers in the world, who are under intense physical and mental pressure, then you can see that its day-to-day benefits for you could be huge.

Finally – and at this point the evidence to support this idea remains anecdotal – there is a growing school of thought that having control over your breathing in this way helps the overall health of your body. It seems logical, really, given that oxygen is one of the very fuels that keeps us all alive. I have had several clients with Irritable Bowel Syndrome who have reported a reduction in symptoms when they have used Zen Breathing daily. Of course, you still need to work with your medical professional on health issues as serious as this, but I look forward to reading the evolving research to see if breathing properly can really be as effective in boosting your health as I think it is.

Going back to the number of breaths we take every day – around twenty-five thousand – this is the only action that your body can perform both subconsciously and consciously. It is therefore easy to see that if we can practise Zen Breathing daily for just five minutes, the benefits will be enormous. At first, try to practise at the same time each day (if possible) as this seems to help establish a routine. Ideally, aim to start with five minutes per session and work up to twenty.

The trick is to practise staying with your Zen Breathing, because it won't be long before you get distracted – that's inevitable. But persevere and you will be delighted with the benefits.

We live in a fast-paced world, so slowing down your breathing is one of the kindest and most helpful things you can do for yourself. If only a fraction of your daily breaths are improved, that is still thousands of times a day that your mind and body will be on the receiving end of fuller, more beneficial breaths surging into you. Of course, I recognize that if you are suffering with anxiety, then asking you to lie quietly and breathe slowly in this fashion might seem a bit of a challenge at first. It might be, but just *start* and give it a go, even for a minute or two. Over the coming days you will see improvements, and before you know it, you will be able to switch on your Zen Breathing easily and successfully in all manner of situations when you need a little assistance.

I must admit that, initially, I felt slightly awkward telling clients about this technique. Some individuals had travelled long distances to see me and all I was doing was telling them how to breathe! However, just because an idea is incredibly simple does not mean it isn't hugely helpful and, secondly, I always kept coming back to the results.

One top rugby player even told me his mental wellbeing had been completely transformed since I taught him to 'breathe like a baby'. I know this advice seems almost obvious, but I promise you that, done correctly, Zen Breathing will change your life.

So go on, find a quiet space, lie down, put your hand on your tummy and give it a go . . .

Zen Breathing
Lord Drayson

Paul Drayson is a highly successful entrepreneur, former Minister of Science in the last Labour government's Department for Business, Innovation and Skills, and also a racing driver. Paul also has the use of only one eye, but that wasn't going to stop him from competing in the Le Mans 24-Hour Race.

Considering all the challenges in his life, it was not remotely surprising that he sought my help not only to keep him safe, but to allow him to be competitive. As Paul himself explains, Zen Breathing was the main Tool he used (among several) to keep himself calm and relaxed, and ready for action on the track. Here is an extract from a speech he gave on 2 March 2011 for the 'Cities of the Future' Industry Forum at the University of Oxford.

I've always loved cars. I grew up near Brands Hatch in Kent and every weekend, if the wind blew in the right direction, I could hear the sound of racing across the valley. My dad used to take me around the paddock in the days when you could get close to the giants of F1. As a teenager, I knew I wanted to be an engineer and work with cars, and in the summer of 2003 I drove my first proper race car – a 1963 AC Cobra – very gingerly around Oulton Park Circuit.

It was one of the scariest experiences of my life – it's a beast of a car and I was hooked. I was forty-three and I wanted to race. And I wanted to race sports cars at the 24 Hours of Le Mans race. If my age wasn't enough of a challenge, I was born blind in one eye – I didn't know it then, but one-eyed drivers weren't allowed to race at Le Mans (how I overcame that is a story for another time). But in spite of all that, I found myself getting my licence, working my way up to second in the British champion- ships, and [then] coming third with my team Drayson Racing in the world series of Le Mans races.

During the past seven years I have been racing, I have learned a few things from some amazing individuals who have really helped me, and I would like to share a few of them with you. I've had the chance to learn how to succeed in high-risk and uncertain situations. Like driving at over 200 mph at night in the rain down the Mulsanne Straight [at Le Mans], where it feels like you've been thrown down a mineshaft holding a torch . . .

How to survive in a scary and uncertain world

So how do you do it? Despite the risks, going out and *still* making it happen?

Now, I know all about being scared and feeling the pressure. The night before the 2010 24 Hours of Le Mans race, I just couldn't sleep. This was very unusual. I normally sleep pretty easily, even before big events, but that fact just made me even more stressed-out lying there. As the hours ticked on, I tried all the usual stuff to get to sleep but it was no use. My mind was running riot and I couldn't stop it. For some bizarre reason, I kept worrying that I was going to miss the pit box during the race and mess everything up. My mind kept re-running the scenario. I kept trying to visualize the key markers as you come down the pit lane – it is so busy it is very easy to miss your stop in the confusion of cars and lights and crews rushing around. Especially at night.

The other nagging worry was rain – and, frankly, crashing. I was scared. A fatality in sports-car racing a few weeks before had put a dent in my confidence. And so this went on all night. My brain fighting with itself just when what it really needed was a good night's sleep.

When I got up next race day morning, sure enough it was raining. A voice in my head – the

Monkey – was saying, 'Maybe it's your intuition telling you not to race, Paul. You know you are a big believer in that. Maybe you are going to have a big crash – end up in hospital, maybe even dead. You are scared for a reason.'

I [had been speaking to Don] and I remember learning quite early on from him that really the Monkey voice is your survival instinct at work. But I knew I couldn't back out – I didn't even want to, but even if I did, I couldn't.

So just a few hours later, I'm standing, fully suited-up, looking down at my feet in the centre of the white ring that marked the fourteenth-placed starting driver's position for the seventy-sixth running of the 24 Hours of Le Mans, before running over to the car for the start.

In the car on the grid, I look in my mirrors and see directly behind me and on the left, the blue-and-red Zytec of former F1 world champion Nigel Mansell! As I'm going through my pre-start routines, a thought slices into my head: 'Mansell is going to do everything he can to catch and pass you, Paul. And if he gets close enough, he could easily put a "do or die" move on you. He wasn't world champion for nothing. His bravery and total commitment were legendary. Better not let him catch me, then.'

I came to racing pretty late and I've had to work very hard to keep up with the professionals who are often half my age, let alone former world champions . . . You have to be relaxed. If you are scared, you are tense and you [then] lose feeling for what the car is doing, and that makes you slow. In motor racing, I've learned how to relax when I'm scared. To perform when under massive pressure.

Last August, we had qualified on pole at Road America – one of the biggest sports-car races in the US. I'd messed up the start of the previous race badly, spun off and nearly wrecked the car, so there was this unspoken worry in the team that I would do it again. And just before the start – when the tank was topped up with fuel – the hose connector had jammed and sprayed race fuel all over me as I was sitting in the car. So there I [was] on pole, with my overalls burning my backside, sitting in a pool of fuel, with everyone half expecting me to mess up again – and the championship in the balance. What did I do?

I did what I'd been taught to do by Don. I focused ahead on the entry into turn one and I breathed very slowly. If there is one thing you take away from tonight, it is this: Zen Breathing works.

When you are *really* under pressure, when you know you have to do it anyway – make that speech, break some bad news, or make a good start in a race – breathe in, counting to three, hold your breath, count to two, breathe out, counting to five. Repeat three times. Your pulse *will* slow down; the adrenalin *will* die down; your muscles *will* relax; your brain *will* be able to think more clearly. You will have energy and things will start to flow.

Trust me. It works.

Frankly, it was a revelation. I've used Zen Breathing many times – speaking in Parliament, even. In fact, I was doing it before I stood up tonight . . .

And I was totally dependent on Don Macpherson. Learning from the best is fundamental. Go after the top talent. The people that really know. Apply their insights.

Good luck. Make the future happen. Thank you.

Tool 2

Mind the Monkey!

How to Think More Positively Using Progressive Language

*'The quality of your thoughts
determines the quality of your life.'*

Having learned how to tune in to your Zen Breathing with Tool 1, you now have the capacity to switch on an overwhelming feeling of beautiful relaxation and calmness whenever you need it. Your Zen Breathing will be an enormous ally in your plan to experience a life full of tranquillity and enjoyment.

However, remember how I warned you that when you practise Zen Breathing, you might sometimes hear your Monkey disturbing that serenity, with all sorts of unhelpful thoughts and ideas that spin around in your head? If allowed to, your Monkey will interrupt and fret at all sorts of times, day and night, not just when you are Zen Breathing. In fact, it will often interject at the worst moment and make a challenging situation much more calamitous. When your Monkey is chattering in this way, it can be very difficult to stay calm, concentrate, sleep well, and not allow your anxiety to get the better of you.

Therefore, it is absolutely crucial to your sense of well-being and enjoyment of life that you develop the ability to Mind the Monkey.

What do I mean by that? Let's take it back to what is happening in your brain all the time. Believe it or not, it is said that we experience around sixty thousand thoughts per day (I'd love to know who counted them), most of which are often regurgitated from previous days – 'on loop', so to speak. Some of these thoughts might be perfectly innocent, such as 'I will take a sip of that coffee now' but some might be 'What am I going to do if I fail that test? It could all go terribly wrong', or 'I think my husband might be ill, he doesn't seem right . . .'

So, although the intensity of your thoughts can vary enormously, the sheer volume of them can mean that it's very easy to become totally overwhelmed. When this happens, it can almost feel as if your Monkey is in charge, that you are just doing what you are told, and reacting to whatever it wants. This is the precise moment when you have to Mind the Monkey – the very essence of mind management. Let me explain . . .

First up, remember this absolutely VITAL FACT: YOU ARE THE BOSS. The real you – the inner you – is the Boss, *not* the Monkey. Although I know it often doesn't feel that way, it is true. You are the Captain, the Monkey is the Co-pilot. The Monkey advises but it is always *you* who has the final say and makes the decisions.

YOU are the Boss.

The secret to Minding the Monkey is knowing that you are in control – once you acknowledge this golden rule, you will be able to take responsibility for your thoughts and change your life. Don't worry, I am not going to tell you to 'think positively'. This might be the single worst platitude that I hear rolled out by people (with admittedly good intentions – see Accidental Mind Coaches on page 217) who are attempting in vain to help others. How can you think positively when your mind is in a fog of anxiety or panic? It's just a slightly more eloquent but ultimately foolish way of telling someone with clinical depression to 'cheer up'. Being positive is relatively easy if everything is hunky-dory in your world, but a damn sight more difficult if you are experiencing some of life's more challenging episodes, such as health worries, concerns about job security or relationship problems.

It's time for you to learn a new language.

Don't worry, I'm not going to ask you to sit down and do a spelling test in French. What we are going to do is *learn the art of Progressive Language*. To do that, we need to take a peep inside your head.

In order to upgrade your mind, first you need accurate awareness of where your thinking is currently, based in terms of positive/negative percentages. To do this you *deliberately* tune in to your own Monkey Chatter. It might seem counter-intuitive, given how I have been saying how unhelpful your Monkey can be, but bear with me, this can often be a very interesting and enlightening experience . . . Ready?

Stop what you are doing (if it is safe to do so) and, if you can, sit or lie down somewhere comfortable. Close your eyes if you wish, but you can also keep them open if you prefer. Now, take a few slow, deep, gentle, peaceful breaths, and turn your attention to what is going on in your head. Shhhh . . . Listen . . . Can you hear it? What is going on in your head, right here, right now?

Don't interfere with the process, just casually observe with childlike curiosity. Tune in. What is the Monkey up to? What is it saying? Is it calm or restless, noisy or quiet? Most importantly, is it in a negative or positive mode? Don't reason or argue with the thoughts . . . just observe them. Keep listening, calmly, and closely monitor this inner dialogue . . .

A quick word of warning: when you first do this, expect to hear a higher proportion of negativity from the Monkey than usual. Some people are surprised at just how negative their Monkey Chatter is, but if this is the case, *don't be alarmed*. This is not unusual, it is the brain's factory setting – its job in this respect is to keep you safe and constantly check if you are OK.

If you hear any negative words, just observe them. Within the negative chatter you will discover all sorts of words that your brain is listening to thousands of times a day, words that make up thoughts that in turn can have a very negative effect on your wellbeing, as well as your view on – and experience of – life. It is precisely these words that we are going to change with Progressive Language.

Let me give you an example from my own personal experience. Some negative thoughts are obvious, such as, 'I really don't think I am good enough to do this', or 'Why am I even thinking of doing this?', but others are much more subtle. When I first sat down to listen to my Monkey Chatter, I observed my inner voice saying, 'I will try', whenever I had a challenge to meet. Sounds all right, doesn't it? But when you really think about it, 'trying' implies an element of self-doubt – it sets you up to fail. If you 'try' to get fit, do you really think you will? If you 'try' to cut back on alcohol, how long do you think that will last? If you invited me for a pint at your local pub and asked to meet at 8 p.m. and I replied, 'I'll try', would you really expect me to turn up?

Once I was aware of my use of the word 'try', I decided instead to replace it with a positive alternative whenever I caught my Monkey saying it. Instead of thinking, *I'll try*, I began to use *I'll do my very best*, or just *I'll give it a go*. Better still, *I will do this*. However, I must admit to finding this supposedly easy task far more difficult than I initially thought it would be. I kept slipping up and was surprised how often 'try' was my default word, even though I'd consciously acknowledged it was not positive enough. However, as with all the techniques in this book, practice makes perfect. Over time I persevered and soon managed to persuade my Monkey Mind that this word was no longer part of *my* mental vocabulary.

This is what I mean by Progressive Language: your choice

of words will enable you to learn to think in a more progressively positive way, by monitoring and identifying negative thoughts that are unjustified, inappropriate, too cautious, too restrictive, too ambiguous. Many of these thoughts and words are well meaning, but ultimately extremely unhelpful, so you have to strip them out of the daily dialogue you have with yourself. Negative words can have a devastating, disempowering, weakening effect on your ability to perform well – in the same way that Kryptonite affects Superman. So it is vital to recognize when your Kryptonite is present, and to unleash the antidote immediately: Progressive Language.

You might find it useful to write down the words and phrases that keep popping up when you are listening to your Monkey Chatter. 'Try' would certainly be on my list. What's on yours? Once you have identified the culprits, write more positive and helpful alternatives next to them. Here are a few examples:

Negative	*Positive*
I can't handle the pressure.	I accept this pressure. Pressure is a privilege.
I worry I will fail.	I surf the waves of worry.
I feel tense and anxious.	I am calm and relaxed.
What if I make a mistake?	There are no mistakes, only learning.

I am not good enough.	I am assertive, I 'can do', and I am confident.
What if I mess up like last time?	There is no last time, only here, now, at this time.
I have butterflies in my tummy.	Butterflies are good – controlled nerves give you focus. Just make sure they are all flying in the right direction.
I don't think I can.	I am well prepared and ready.
I always wrestle and struggle with my life.	My life is a dance, and I am dancing.
I am such a worrier.	I face all my concerns and float with them.
I am so unlucky. Poor me.	Today is my lucky day and I am grateful for the chance.
No!	Yes!
Can't!	Can!

Keep your piece of paper with you and have a quick look at it whenever you hear those negative words and phrases popping into your head. Remind yourself of your preferred alternatives and practise using them. Changing your words and thoughts into more positive ones is a mental skill and, just like with all skills, the more you practise, the better you become.

What you are now doing is not just using different, more Progressive Language, *you are controlling your thinking.* You are learning to Mind the Monkey. This relatively simple Tool is a hugely powerful skill that will enable you to turn the overall balance of thoughts in your brain in favour of the positives, rather than the negatives. Some brain experts believe that you need to drown out unwanted persistent negative thoughts with positive ones by a ratio of 5:1, the reason being that negative ideas are stronger because of their frequently over-protective nature. So you have work to do – but don't 'try', just crack on.

The more you let negative thoughts roam freely in your mind, the more powerful they become. It is therefore essential to interrupt this process before the negatives find their way into your subconscious where they will be harder to shift or change. So here's a technique to transform your vocabulary into one filled with Progressive Language: *Zap the Monkey!*

What I mean by this is, do not attempt to suppress or deny your negative thoughts, simply be aware of them and then *zap* them with a more positive word or thought as quickly as you can. Do this every time a negative word or phrase that you have highlighted pops up. *Quick! Zap the Monkey!* Have some fun, turn it into a game as you swat and bat away the negative words and thoughts. If you practise zapping the negative words with a powerful, positive alternative, they will never make it as far as your subconscious. *Zap! Biff! Zap!* If you can end up smiling, or maybe even laughing occasionally when you Zap the Monkey, then you are making massive progress.

Another approach that some of my clients like to take is to imagine a TV remote control. If you were to switch on your television because your favourite show is about to start, but another channel comes on instead, showing the worst programme you could imagine, what would you do? You would grab the remote control as fast as you could, and change the channel *tout de suite*! Do the same with your thoughts. Whenever you tune in to your awareness of what your Monkey Mind is saying to you, as soon as you realize a word is not at all appropriate or helpful, find the remote control and change channel to your preferred choice as quickly as you can.

Remember, you are not striving for a complete removal of all negativity. To be fair to the Monkey, its 'don't do that' advice may well save your life – for example, if you are about to step out into busy traffic without looking first! No, it is more about rebalancing your thinking in favour of positivity. Progressive Language stops negative thoughts from dominating, overwhelming and drowning the positive words and thoughts. In extreme cases, full-blown phobias and mental health crises can develop if negative words and thoughts are allowed to go unchecked, but even if your situation is less acute, you still need to make better choices with your internal language.

Progressive Language is your mental programme to stop negative words and thoughts in their tracks. It is all about teaching your Monkey Mind to switch to more positive alternatives and to challenge the validity of all negative (or even 'wishy-washy') words as soon as you become aware of them. The more you practise Progressive Language the more positive you will actually become. It is what winners do, even though they might not be aware they are doing it.

Let me give you an example from the world of tennis, a world I have spent many years working in. Novak Djokovic, the world's number-one player, has learned to master his Monkey Mind by changing negative words into 'can-do' words. For some time he was as physically fit as any other tennis player, and arguably as technically sound, yet for several years he was stuck at around third in the world rankings. Then he realized there was only one more thing to take care of: he tuned his brain for better, more positive thinking. He did this by using language in his inner dialogue that was rampantly positive, empowering and fuelling his confidence in his ability. It allowed him to stoke the fire of self-belief, which he acknowledges is the main reason he was able to reach the top spot in the world tennis rankings and become one of the greatest players of all time. Djokovic became fluent in Progressive Positive Language . . . You can, too.

Now that you have started your own Progressive Language course, let's help you fast-track that new vocabulary. How? By introducing the concept of mantras. Now, before you flick past this page thinking, *He is going to ask me to do yoga next*, don't worry, I won't!

The word mantra, borrowed from Sanskrit, means 'mind tool' – 'man' (mind) and 'tra' (tool). The history books tell us that mantras originate as far back as 3000 BC, and are often found deeply rooted in Buddhist, Hindu and Sikh scriptures. Mantras are classed as a 'sacred utterance', and can be a single word, a few words or even a short verse. They can be spoken aloud or to oneself. Depending on individual circumstances, mantras can be said once or repeated often.

They are exceptionally good at blocking negative thoughts, words and feelings. For that reason, I call them Monkey Blockers. For example, let's look at one of the most famous of all modern mantras, Muhammad Ali's 'I am the greatest'. He kept on repeating this phrase way before he actually became the greatest boxer in the world, and it worked because it totally blocked his (understandably) stressed-out, worried Monkey Mind. Ali was facing some of the most dangerous, violent and feared boxers ever to climb inside a ring, so it was only reasonable that his Monkey Mind would have been alarmed and filled his head with 'what ifs'. Ali didn't listen, though. He kept telling everybody – including himself – that he was 'the greatest' and, in time, that's exactly what he became.

Your own mantra(s) can be very personal to you, but to get you started, take a look back at the negative/positive phrases that I highlighted earlier in this chapter on pages 56–7 and consider using some of the latter. Another source of inspiration could be a mantra I find top sportspeople using all the time: 'Lock in'. I know several world-class sporting personalities who say these words to themselves over and over again in challenging situations, and report back that it really focuses their mind on a particular task with remarkable clarity. 'Lock in' means to lock in *only* to the process of what you are doing, not the result. In sport this may also be called a 'trigger', to ensure complete focus is on the task in hand, not the outcome, therefore blocking any negative Monkey Chatter.

Whatever wording you choose to use, remember that your mantra can be spoken out loud or to yourself and repeated as often as you like – an additional benefit of reciting your mantra is that it is impossible to hear the Monkey when you are doing so. It's a bit like when a child puts their hands over their ears when they are being told off; you are using your mantra to block the Monkey Chatter.

Don't worry, you don't have to be a Tibetan monk and sit halfway up a mountain to use mantras to your benefit. When added to your new Progressive Language and your fresh awareness of what your Monkey Chatter is actually saying, mantras will complete an exceptionally potent trio of techniques that will help to transform your outlook on life.

One final, fun tip about the power of Progressive Language in helping to diffuse and control your Monkey: at some point – I don't honestly remember when or why – I started to call my monkey Mike. I even bought a large, cuddly, stuffed toy who, to this day, sits on top of my office couch. I introduce Mike to everyone who comes to see me, and often take it into schools, universities and sports clubs when I give talks. It is a great way to break the ice and makes people smile, immediately creating a much more light-hearted atmosphere.

To my surprise and delight, after they had met my Mike, several clients started to give their own monkeys names, too! I soon realized that this was of significant benefit in helping them relate to their inner dialogue in a more friendly, accessible way, and in accelerating the process of being more in control of their monkey chatter, thoughts and emotions. I started to encourage more and more of my clients to name their monkeys, because the feedback I was getting was that it really did allow them to see issues and challenges from another angle, and to give things fresh meaning and perspective. And, yes, more than a few of my clients have also bought their own stuffed monkeys! The names these monkeys have been given are often highly creative, always amusing and sometimes very insightful! Here are a few I remember with great fondness: Jeremy, Martha, Madge, Vince, Ezmerelda, Colin, Morris, Ninja, Bruce, Maximus, Boris, Franko, Malcolm, Deirdre, Godfrey, Roger and even Corporal Jones. Try this yourself as a fun idea – you can do so knowing that naming your Monkey is in fact a very powerful tool in itself. I am sure it will make you smile, too.

*

The Tools

Here is a reminder of the three steps of learning Progressive Language:

1. Tune in to your inner voice to identify the inappropriate negative words and phrases you hear, and increase your awareness of them.
2. Zap them with lots of positive alternatives.
3. Accelerate the process by using your mantra(s).

Progressive Language will also allow you to be a more positive and therefore more confident person. When you are more confident, you automatically become more capable (see also Tool 4: Hollywood Movie – page 87), whatever the size of the challenge you are facing, and are therefore far more likely to reap the rewards that all your efforts and hard work deserve.

Millions of people around the world learn a new language every year, they enjoy the process and it makes them feel good – I have a GCSE in Japanese! Learning a language is a wonderful experience – and that is what you are going to do with your new knowledge and application of Progressive Language. Before you know it, your head will be swimming with positive words and ideas, and any negatives will be zapped before they can take hold. Before long, you will be choosing those alternative words instinctively – the ultimate goal of learning any language. Soon you will be fluent in Progressive Language and when you are, your life will be *transformed*.

Let's do it.

Mind the Monkey!

Zak

Zak is a tall, good-looking, polite and pleasant young man, and a fine rugby player. Like many teenagers, he came to see me during a period of his life when he needed direction and mentoring. His father was concerned Zak had lost his enthusiasm for rugby and playing his guitar; in fact, for life in general. I could see very quickly that Zak had a lot of potential, on and off the rugby pitch. His story will inspire every teenager who might have lost their way a bit – so remember, like Zak, and indeed myself when I was a teen, that all those who wander are not lost. Zak made use of the Zen Breathing technique to give himself a safe, calm place to regain some mental energy, and to reconnect to his enthusiasm for rugby and playing his guitar, but Mind the Monkey became his main Tool.

I met Don in the summer of 2015, following a successful rugby tournament with my school team.

Unbeknown to everyone at the competition, including my family, I was not enjoying the success at all. My experiences prior to the 2015 tournament were no different to those of any aspiring rugby player who had been successful at this point in his career. From the outside, I'm sure it looked great. However, my Monkey Mind was slowly eating away at me. I thought I was the only one going through this, however, Don's teachings have proved otherwise.

I had a successful school career. I earned two rugby scholarships, was a member of the Bath Rugby Academy and had represented the South West U16. The best examples I can share about my journey – and hopefully the most relatable experiences – come from my time at Bath Rugby. Up to that point, I had been thoroughly enjoying my successes and time on the field, playing alongside close friends from school. Things changed when an immense amount of pressure was thrust upon me, from the Monkey and from Bath Academy. All of a sudden, fifteen-year-old me was thrown into a professional set-up, with professional expectations.

The pressure and stresses tore me apart – I stopped enjoying rugby full stop. I dreaded the residential camps – heaven forbid I should be selected for a tournament! I couldn't even watch matches on TV. I'd get so wound up before training sessions and games that I would actually seek to avoid them. Most vividly, I remember skipping one U16 tournament when I actually got my dad to phone in for me! This was a textbook Monkey Sabotage.

I moved to a new school during this unstable period at Bath Rugby, and what an upset that was. Not only did I move to an entirely new environment, but I also moved to a full-on rugby programme. Bath Academy hosted training sessions every Monday, and all I could think about was how to get out of them. To cut a long story short, before Christmas that year I nearly left that school. My Monkey was so firmly in control that I was not in a good place. I was meeting with my tutor and housemaster multiple times a week, but could not pinpoint the reasons why I was feeling the way I was.

School life improved in the second half of the year as the rugby season tapered off. I enjoyed athletics in the summer as there was no expectation on me and the academy season had finished. We made it to the semi-finals of a big tournament unexpectedly, but for a final time I was sabotaged by my Monkey Mind. This was the turning point for me, and the first time I'd opened up to my dad about how I was feeling. I was at my lowest point.

Dad contacted Don that summer. I didn't hold out much hope – he'd found this bloke out of the blue and arranged a meeting. We nipped over to Bath for my session with Don. I was slightly dubious as to where this was going, given that this strange man would refer to the Monkey Mind and point to his pet toy monkey, which was called Mike and was sat on the sofa. Nevertheless, I was desperate to get out of the hole I was in, and so I gave it my all. Several more sessions with Don followed. The time I spent with him changed my life.

Zak's Monkey Mind had become frustrated and increasingly agitated, to the point of basically running Zak's life without him knowing it. Zen Breathing brought Zak some clarity, and calmed his Monkey enough for him to see the way forward, reclaim control of his thoughts, his emotions and his life. He was able to challenge the Monkey's negative chatter, see the true meaning of things and put them in perspective.

Best Zak

After a summer with Don, we had crafted 'Best Zak'. I was equipped to Mind the Monkey . . . For the first time in three years I could not wait to get on the rugby pitch again. Our first game of the season is always a big one – 'Pilgrims' as it's known to the local boys. All the old boys would return for the match – there was probably a crowd of a good four hundred people! We were due to meet at the pitch at 1.30 p.m. to warm up. I had just finished Saturday's lessons and got back into bed to go through my new pre-match routine (as I would for every home game that followed thereafter), when our replacement prop burst into my dorm. He was sweating profusely, out of breath and ranting about how nervous he was – yet there I was, in bed, energized and excited to get to the pitch!

We had an incredibly successful season, one of the best the school had seen in more than twenty years. I was made vice-captain of the First XV, captain of the First VII, and won school colours. I went on to become head of house and a school prefect (very unusual for a sixth-form import).

Even Better Zak

Before I left school, I was let go by Bath Rugby. This didn't bother me at all, as I was in the best place mentally that I'd ever been! I went on to secure a place at one of the top high schools near Chicago, to coach and play for a season. This is when my time with Don got really exciting. 'Best Zak' was now embarking on chapter two of my Mind the Monkey journey, so Don and I set out to craft an 'Even Better Zak'. A summer of sessions and training brought us to January 2017 when I set off on my adventure.

A month into my American experience, my teammate, who had accompanied me from home, decided to leave. This left me alone in the States and was a daunting time for me, but I knew I had never been so well-equipped for the job. Two games in, I was made captain of the varsity side, but received a blow when I ruptured a ligament in my right ankle. I was side-lined for eight weeks – another hurdle to overcome – but I returned to play and led Penn High School to win the Midwest Championship, and become number two in the US League table. We defeated the number-one team in the US and narrowly missed out on the State Championship.

The Next Chapter

During my time in the States, my dad had been involved in a business dispute. I could see the Monkey taking control of Dad and leading him to a place I knew too well. At the time, I was in close contact with Don, and between us we got my father back on track. Being able to help someone who had been there for me all those years before was the most rewarding part of going through this process, and I see it as the pinnacle of that particular stage in my life. I'd gone from the lowest of lows to recognizing and helping someone who was facing the same battles with their Monkey that I had experienced for all those years.

I owe a great deal to Don. He revived my love for rugby and gave me the Tools to become one of life's warriors. Tools that not only turned my life around but also enabled me to help others. No matter where I am or what I do now, I know I have the ability to Mind the Monkey, and that gives me a mental edge, an incredibly powerful mindset to have.

Tool 3

The Kaizen

How to Always Improve

*'Kaizen means improvement. Moreover, it means
continuing improvement in personal life, home life,
social life and working life. Improving the world with
everyone, everywhere, every day – The Kaizen Way.'*

Masaaki Imai, organisational theorist and author of
Kaizen: The Key to Japan's Competitive Success

You might think that meeting a three-time Formula One
world champion had enough of an impact on my life in itself.
Well, as I mentioned, Sir Jack Brabham OBE was a long-
standing and good friend. More pertinently, he introduced
me to a close friend of his, Nobuhiko Kawamoto, who was
not only the president of Honda from 1990 to 1998, but also
the boss of that manufacturer's Formula One motor-racing
activities. It just so happened that Honda was dominating
F1 during that time, in partnership with the McLaren F1

team and their super-talented – indeed, legendary – driver Ayrton Senna.

Thanks to Sir Jack, I was given access to areas of Honda Motor Company and introduced to influential decision-makers, and quickly came to the conclusion that learning about Japanese culture, history, philosophy and its beautiful language might be a good idea. I studied Japanese avidly and enjoy speaking that ancient tongue to this day. I also visited Japan on many occasions to work with Formula One racing teams, several Japanese racing drivers, and large corporations such as Yamaha, Nissan, Toshiba, Fujifilm and, of course, Honda. More crucially, I also became fascinated with the Japanese 'Zen of life', and it wasn't long before I came across a simple but incredibly powerful concept called 'the Kaizen', which can be translated as meaning 'continuous change for the better'.

'Kai' = change
'Zen' = better

So, what exactly is the Kaizen?

The Kaizen is the concept of continual, small improvements – finding an area of your life that you want to improve, and then taking positive steps every day, even if it is only in a tiny way. Not great big elephant strides, but the much smaller steps of a dancer. There is a real simplicity and beauty in this idea, and it is something that I have studied and made a central part of my life ever since I first learned of it.

The reason the concept works so well with our Monkey Mind is precisely because the improvements are *small*. As a result, the interfering Monkey doesn't notice that you are indeed making changes 'for the better'. You are sneaking under its radar, so the Monkey simply lets you get on with things without going into meltdown and refusing to cooperate. Remember, your Monkey only has two jobs – the main one is to keep you safe, but it is also there to stop you from making an arse of yourself – and it will often go to great lengths to 'carry out its duties'.

One of your Monkey's favourite methods of monitoring what you are doing and how you are doing it – *basically checking up on you* – is to keep you in a comfortable world, nice and cosy and safe, a completely risk-free zone away from any potential danger. It does sound rather nice being in a comfort zone, doesn't it? Well, that may be fine and dandy if you are lying on a beach sipping a cocktail on holiday, but not at all helpful if you are attempting to make significant long-term changes to your life. And make no mistake, if you attempt to make sudden big leaps towards change, then sure enough, your Monkey will be rattled. The negative consequences will be almost immediate and ultimately debilitating.

The theories of the Monkey Mind and the Kaizen are sublimely complementary; they are two profoundly powerful Tools that will help you to make long-lasting and impactful changes to your life, as well as bringing many benefits to your health and keeping you firmly on the road to Success City.

I began applying the Kaizen to my own life and the results were dramatic. The same can happen for you. The Kaizen Tool allows you to choose something that you really want to be better at, and as a consequence be more successful with. It can be absolutely anything. I am sure you can think of something, such as:

1. Being healthier, perhaps by reducing your weight
2. Enjoying socializing more
3. Speaking in public
4. Passing exams or tests of any kind
5. Finding a partner
6. Forging a better relationship, if you already have a partner
7. Making progress at work through promotion
8. Getting fitter by increasing the amount of exercise you do
9. Being calmer and less anxious, by living your life more in the present

Sounds good? Let's have a closer look at the Kaizen in action.

First, a quick story of gross misuse of the Kaizen (how not to do it) . . . by me!

For as long as I can remember, I have always had a problem with standing at the top of tall buildings or high cliffs. When I get close to the edge, I get a weird feeling of being drawn, almost pulled over the side – the very last thing I intend or want to do! This feeling is usually accompanied by some dizziness and nausea. I obviously have some form of vertigo (there seem to be several), more commonly known as a fear of heights . . . and this is how I clumsily attempted to fix it in my pre-Kaizen days.

My friend, the musician Peter Gabriel, knew about my fear of heights and one day, completely out of the blue, he called and said, 'Right! Richard Branson is sending me one of his Virgin hot-air balloons. I thought you might like to come up with me – it will sort out your "heights thing" once and for all, I reckon.' He then added, 'I'll give you twenty minutes to decide if you want to do it – call me back . . .'

How could I refuse? It was certainly going to be kill or cure, so up, up and away we went. Richard Branson wasn't personally piloting the heavily liveried corporate red balloon (which came as something of a relief), but the basket was a lot smaller than I had anticipated, which was less of a relief.

For Peter, who couldn't care less about heights, it was an unforgettable experience with wonderful panoramic views of Glastonbury Tor and the beautiful West Country landscape. Me? Alas, all I could do was crouch down as low as I could in the bottom of the basket, hanging on grimly to a sturdy rope with all my agitated strength, focusing entirely on my white-knuckle grip. The edge of the basket seemed too low for my (and my Monkey's) liking, so my anxiety was really severe. To be perfectly honest, it frightened the bloody life out of me, to the point where I swore that no amount of money or other method of persuasion would ever get me up in another balloon again. In short, my Monkey went into overdrive, its safety catch was undone, and as a result the entire experience was somewhat less than enjoyable!

Had I used the Kaizen before my balloon trip, my experience would have been entirely different: this Tool really is that powerful. Let me illustrate the Kaizen by using the 'builder's plank' example to demonstrate how it can engineer an escape from your own Monkey Mind's over-protective control.

Imagine a sturdy builder's plank of wood, roughly 12 feet long, about 2 feet off the ground, bridging the gap between two low, stone walls. If I were to ask you to walk along the plank, do you think you could do it? Of course you could! In fact, you could probably do it blindfolded. Now, imagine that same plank of wood, but this time it is positioned much higher – between two buildings, 100 feet off the ground. That would certainly be enough to provoke some interference from my Monkey, Mike ('What the hell are you thinking? Are you crazy?'). What height might elicit a similar response from your Monkey Mind? Higher? Lower? What would your answer be now if I were to ask you to 'walk the plank'?

In reality, you really should be able to walk the second plank just as easily as the first, because the physical motor skills required to do so are the same, aren't they? What's changed? Yes, you're right, it's more Monkey Business! Down on the plank between the two stone walls, you didn't hear the Monkey in your head at all. You simply focused on putting one foot in front of the other. You totally trusted your balance and reached the other side. Easy-peasy.

However, if you did attempt to cross the plank at a greater height, you'd almost certainly hear the Monkey screaming at you to get the hell down before you fell off and killed yourself. Unfortunately, with this din going on inside your head, it would be impossible to concentrate on the process of walking along the plank. And to be fair to the Monkey, it would only be doing its job – which is to keep you safe. In order to do so, it would flood your body with a veritable tsunami of adrenalin and you'd rapidly start to lose control of most of your motor skills, as well as your sense of balance, while your head filled with self-doubt and a strong desire to look for the nearest lift back to terra firma!

I am not saying I could ever walk this particular walk, but imagine if I had to? Perhaps one night, after imbibing more Japanese whisky than was sensible, I might open my big mouth and say, 'Bring it on,' when challenged to do so by one of my five grandkids – yikes! Now what? How the heck am I going to persuade Mike to let me do it?

Well, there are two complementary ways that work in tandem.

First, bribe Mike with a substantial sum of money, which

would be donated to one of my favourite charities on completion of the challenge. Mike would still be anything but thrilled about it, but would have to concede there was now a good reason for me to have a go, and would therefore be far more likely to let me get on with the process of 'just doing it'.

Second, use the Kaizen. So, how exactly is the Kaizen going to help me do this?

It's quite simple, really – and that in itself is one of the most powerful aspects of the Kaizen Tool. I would repeat the walk again and again, but would very gradually increase the height of the plank each time – inch by inch, if necessary – all the way up to the highest point. In this way, I would be challenging my vertigo/fear of heights little by little, and as my confidence grew and improvements became more evident, I would have the option to accelerate my progress . . . but not to the degree where I might get carried away and end up self-sabotaging. Always baby steps, onwards and upwards I'd go, without Mike even noticing I'm on my way up – literally!

Another Kaizen in action in my own life was when I reluctantly had to concede that my Monkey Mind had come to control my alcohol consumption too much (Monkeys like rewards!). Somehow my intake had crept up to a weekly limit my doctor thought was 'not helpful' to my health and wellbeing, and so he advised a reduction. Dry January was being advertised everywhere at the time (although I didn't meet a single person who was actually participating).

'Cut it out!' – completely, overnight, for a whole month – shouted dozens of headlines. The problem was, when my Monkey heard that I was considering going dry for a whole month, he went completely bananas and told me in no uncertain terms there was no way he would allow that. I battled hard against that, to be fair: I did some meditation, and in a quieter moment asked the Monkey why I had no chance of succeeding with the Dry January plan, but his arguments were very convincing and so I had to reluctantly agree he was probably right. Stopping drinking would not happen if I went 'all out'.

So I suggested to my Monkey that Japanese whisky could be left on the evening menu. He agreed immediately that this was indeed a very cunning plan that he could support. I bought a proper measuring cup (so as not to over-pour), then made sure that each subsequent glass of Yamazaki or Hibiki contained a fraction less than the previous glass . . . until my weekly units were 'more acceptable' to the medical experts (and, you'll be pleased to hear, they still are!). And my Monkey never even noticed . . .

Let's expand this idea into one of the biggest single areas that people in modern society seem to struggle with – food! The Kaizen is particularly effective when your Monkey has 'got you in a hairy headlock' and won't let go with regards to food.

Put yourself in the Monkey's shoes (yes, I know they don't wear shoes, but you get my drift). This little Monkey has been enjoying chocolate and cakes whenever it feels fed up, stressed or anxious. The treats taste great and they induce that all-important, longed-for dopamine hit. The Monkey likes the way that food makes it feel. Simple.

Then, all of a sudden – let's say on 2 January – the Monkey hears some very worrying news: from now on, there will be no crisps, chocolate, bread, potatoes or (oh, blimey) alcohol for weeks – possibly months. A full-on, off-the-cliff-face 'resolution' to eat more healthily has arrived.

Does the Monkey throw a tantrum and refuse to cooperate? No, because your Monkey is a crafty little so-and-so. It will go along with this harsh new regime for a while – a few days, weeks, maybe even a month or two. However, in reality, your Monkey is waiting in the shadows to sabotage this new world and take back control. When the Monkey does exactly that – which it will – and you've had the first piece of cake in six weeks, it will spend all its energy reminding you that you might as well have a few biscuits, or a glass of wine . . . Before you know it, you're feeling bad about yourself and your good intentions are ruined. Meanwhile, the Monkey is slumped in a chair, rubbing a belly full of sweets and cakes and chocolates, delighted.

This is why applying the Kaizen to your relationship with food works. Don't stop eating the things you like. Just eat less of them. You can plan this carefully if that suits you, so that you gradually reduce the levels of the foods that are causing the problems. You also gradually change how you talk about and behave around food.

That's why I never tell people that they need to 'lose'

weight. The Monkey likes to be in control and does not like losing anything. If it suspects that it might be about to lose something, then it will panic and the process suddenly becomes much tougher. Instead, I tell people they might want to 'reduce' their weight. A small but not insignificant difference.

You will be amazed at how other seemingly small changes with the Kaizen can transform your relationship with food. Your Monkey will not panic, it will barely notice the small changes. Essentially, you can do a deal with your Monkey friend . . . and in so doing, start to take back control of what you eat.

These examples might not apply to the areas of your world that you want to improve but remember, the Kaizen will work for *any* area of your life. Choose the specific goal you have, then have a calm think about how that might be reached using the Kaizen approach: tiny steps, gradually, slowly, almost imperceptibly, but always moving forward.

The Kaizen is the accelerator for your potential as well as your Comfort-zone Buster. It is your mental Tool to improve any aspect of your life – albeit gradually, but inexorably and confidently – and to become more successful. Crucially, let the Kaizen keep you focused on the process of progress, not the result and goals. Small changes can bring you big rewards, just as small drops of rain falling consistently on stone can change landscapes over time.

The Kaizen is one small step for the Monkey, one giant leap towards your success . . .

Case Study

The Kaizen

Megan

Megan's dad is a good friend of mine, and he and Megan's mum had become very concerned that their daughter was losing too much weight and not eating as healthily as she should have been. So Dad brought her down to see me, and we went to work. Megan was a 'normal' teenager, doing well at school, and was particularly good at athletics. So what was going on? It soon became obvious that her Monkey Mind had sabotaged her food intake and put a complete block on anything it considered to be 'fattening', especially all the fun stuff such as chocolate, doughnuts, and so on.

As you will see, Megan did a great job in reclaiming control of her eating habits. She used the Mind the Monkey Tool in order to challenge the Monkey's views on what she should be eating, but the main Tool for her was the Kaizen. Very gradually – mouthful by mouthful, meal by meal, day by day – she increased her intake of food to the point that the real Megan – the Inner Megan – knew what was good for her . . . eventually even allowing herself the occasional treat.

Throughout my early teenage years I struggled a lot with body confidence. I didn't like my body and I always felt very unhappy with the way that I looked. I therefore made a decision that I would change my body so I would feel happier within myself. This began very innocently by choosing to eat healthily and exercising more. However, this soon spiralled out of control. I began reducing meal sizes and exercising more and more until my weight was dropping dramatically.

This downward spiral was led by the voice in my head presenting a different image in my mind to what was actually a very unhealthy reality. It was a hugely negative period, which greatly affected my confidence and impacted my family as they could see how my actions were destroying my health. I knew this was something I had to deal with, and only I could help myself recover.

When my dad took me to see Don, it was a turning point. I gained a new perspective about what was happening in my mind – it gave me the opportunity to regain control. Don told me about the Monkey. I realized it was the Monkey who was filling my mind with negative thoughts about myself, and I had allowed it to escape from its cage. It was down to me to put the Monkey back in that cage and regain control of the situation.

This was easier said than done. Although I knew what I had to do in order to combat the Monkey, food still remained a challenge. However, a pivotal moment was the realization of how weak my body had become. For me, sport has always been a very big and important part of my life, and being physically fit was a necessity. However, because of my poor relationship with food I had become weak. I feared not being able to keep up with my netball team and not being able to play at all, which kickstarted a huge change in attitude. It was like I'd flicked a switch in my head. I wanted to be strong and in control rather than be controlled by the Monkey.

I began giving myself more freedom with my food. I started to allow myself the things that I loved, which I would usually have denied myself – like chocolate! At long last I could relax around food. I did much of this by applying the Kaizen, which gave me a softly-softly approach to changing my relationship with food and really helped.

Now I am eighteen and have just completed my A levels. I'm hoping to study psychology at

Loughborough University. Since overcoming anorexia I have a new-found respect and love for my body, and how strong and capable it is. I have never felt more confident with my body as I have in recent years. Obviously, everyone has insecurities and days when they feel they don't look as good; however, now I know how to cage my Monkey – those thoughts and feelings don't consume me.

When Don asked me to write about my experience I had to think really hard about what I was going through and feeling at that point in my life, because now I don't think about what I eat – I enjoy food freely without a second thought. Looking back on how much I struggled, I'm filled with an overwhelming sense of pride about my recovery. Managing your own mind is a challenge, and for a long while I was my biggest enemy. Now I understand and believe that I am my biggest advocate.

Tool 4

Hollywood Movie

How to Be More Confident

Personally, I don't believe anyone is born with in-built confidence, just as I find it difficult to accept a champion is born a champion. My experiences of working with winners (in and out of the sporting arena) is that their success is down to nurture far more than nature. I am referring specifically to the brain here, as it is obvious that genetics play a vital role in a person's *physical* ability to achieve their goals, especially when it comes to sports.

For example, as I am somewhat vertically challenged, I very much doubt that I'd ever win an Olympic gold medal for the high jump! Likewise, in modern tennis, if you are not at least 6 feet 2 inches (for men) or more than 5 feet 7 inches (for women), you could be at a serious disadvantage.

Physical attributes aside, in my opinion, genuine confidence comes from a feeling *inside* you of being centred, grounded and balanced. Who you really are – the Inner

You. This creates a self-awareness that you are *not* the Monkey, you are *not* your thoughts and emotions; you are the Boss, *the Monkey works for you.* You are the Captain, the Monkey is your Co-pilot. Never forget that.

I know from personal experience that life often doesn't feel this way. An over-protective, meddling Monkey is the main reason that your confidence may not be as strong as it could be. My Monkey (Mike) interferes with my confidence levels all too often: questioning, doubting, criticizing, checking. *Am I good enough? Am I fully prepared? Do I remember how I messed up last time? Is it dangerous? Am I safe? Can I be trusted?* Yes, the Monkey is doing its job, but it's not always helpful when it comes to confidence, is it?

Unlike my vertically challenged stature, your confidence is something you *can* change. So, to begin with, take that important fact and ponder it for a moment. If you feel you are under-confident or think your life could be so much more rewarding if your confidence levels were different, then I have some great news – you are about to start to change that. Let's have a look at how your confidence can be nurtured and boosted massively. Let me introduce you to the Hollywood Movie Tool.

Many champions from the world of sport have confirmed how much value they place on using specific visualization techniques to help them boost their confidence and ensure they are able to give their best, whatever challenges they face. In my opinion, no one has articulated it as beautifully and as accurately as Jack Nicklaus, who without doubt was one of the greatest golfers of all time:

> I never hit a shot, even in practice, without having an in-focus, clear picture of it in my head. It's like a colour movie. I see the ball exactly where I want it to finish – nice and white and sitting up high on the bright green grass. Then the scene changes. I 'see' the ball 'going there' – its path, trajectory, shape, even its behaviour on landing.

What Jack is articulating here can be summed up in a variety of catchphrases such as 'What you can SEE you can BE' and 'What you can VIEW you can DO'. Scientific research backs this up. Many research studies by top universities and eminent neuroscientists have concluded that, when used correctly, mental rehearsal using special visualization techniques can boost your confidence significantly and create a powerful feeling of being totally prepared.

Of course, visualization techniques and mental rehearsal is anything but new. In 1940s France, a complex of caves was discovered, on the walls and ceilings of which were paintings and drawings of large animals dating back some seventeen thousand years. Many depicted spears soaring through the air in the general direction of the poor beasts, clearly recording past hunting expeditions for food and reminding the cavemen of their success. This meant that the last thing the hunter-gatherers saw as they left the safety of the warm fire were powerful images of a successful hunting outcome. With their confidence now turbo-charged, they could head off in search of food.

In such wild and dangerous times, any boost of confidence could mean the difference between life and death. Of course, the cavemen were not consciously practising mind management, but in essence that was what those pictures were helping them do.

I believe this is why sports teams often make their dressing rooms 'cave-like', plastering the walls with large photos of past glories and successes. You frequently see the corridors leading to the pitch adorned with more photos of the home team's glorious achievements, no doubt also creating a somewhat more negative effect in the opposition . . . Confidence can, of course, work both ways. Essentially, these athletes and sports stars are much like the cavemen of seventeen thousand years ago, boosting their confidence right up to the last second of leaving the warmth and safety of their relative comfort zones before heading into battle.

The question is, how can you use the Hollywood Movie Tool to similarly turbo-boost your confidence?

If it all sounds tricky, then let me assure you that you probably already practise this mental Tool – in fact, we all do. Daydreaming is a form of mental rehearsal, and who doesn't do that?

I should know, I did plenty of it at school, until I was rudely brought back to the present by a teacher yelling,

'Macpherson! Stop gawping out of the window and concentrate on the blackboard!' If it was in Woodwork, the wake-up call would often be accompanied by a large chunk of timber hurtling towards my head! I used to mentally rehearse throwing that wood back at the 'teacher', but of course I never did.

However, my point still stands. Drifting off, playing out a scenario in your mind, imagining events as they might happen in the future – sometimes in the tiniest detail – we all do this every day. But *none of it actually happens*, we are just visualizing it.

In truth, everyone has the power to visualize. We can all mentally rehearse being the best version of ourselves, whatever challenges we are facing. The key to my version of this idea – the Hollywood Movie Tool – is to become more adept at visualization so that you can use the technique to its absolute maximum benefit.

Some people are better at visualization than others, but I have found that this is mainly because they have practised more often and simply become more proficient. A mental skill is just like any technical skill, such as playing a musical instrument: the more you practise the better you get. The Hollywood Movie technique is a Tool you can practise and improve at – and the ultimate reward is that as you become more adept, your confidence will grow and grow.

We can do better than just daydream; by using and practising special visualization techniques we can *super-charge* the process, leading to fantastic benefits.

Here is what I do when it comes to speaking in public, which has often been a challenge for me personally. Even though I have delivered many talks, I still get nervous when I lecture at schools or universities, and I know that I am not alone – public speaking is many people's worst nightmare. In fact, it regularly appears in the top five phobias. It even has its own quaint, but rather odd, clinical name: glossophobia.

Whenever I have a speaking engagement on the horizon, I apply the Hollywood Movie Tool. As the day in question looms ever nearer, my Monkey Mind starts to rev up and grow louder, with the intention of making sure I don't mess up and make an arse of myself. In order to soothe the Monkey's furrowed brow, I remind Mike I've done plenty of similar talks before, but this isn't usually enough to pacify him.

So I take him to the cinema to watch my latest Hollywood blockbuster: *Goodbye, Glossophobia*. My movie is about to start . . . but first I need to find somewhere nice and comfy where I can safely close my eyes and not be disturbed for the next twenty minutes or so, because the cinema is *inside my head*.

With my eyes closed, I now get extra comfy in whatever it is I am resting on, scratch whatever I need to scratch, then keep my body absolutely still . . . Now, and only now, can I turn my attention to my breath and switch on the Zen Breathing. I tell it to slow down, slow . . . down. You need your breathing to be calm in order to make the most of your Hollywood Movie.

At this stage, only my tummy should be moving, gently

up and down, as the Zen Breathing technique begins to work its magic. Soon, I sense a wonderful peace and calm moving through my body, from the top of my head to my toes. I am in control of my emotions and my thoughts more and more, and the Monkey Chatter gradually fades until it is nothing more than a whisper.

OK, let's make this challenge as difficult as possible – let's imagine I have been asked to be best man at a close friend's wedding!

The brain loves to have a target, so the first phase of this Tool is to give it one: I need to see myself from a bird's-eye view, from above. In neuroscience circles this is what is known as 'third-person visualization' and it works really well to crystallize a desired outcome.

From my elevated position, I picture myself at the top table, dressed appropriately for the wedding. I can see all the guests clearly as I wait calmly for my turn to give the speech. The images are all in high definition, rich in detail with vivid colour. I continue to watch myself from the bird's-eye view as I rise from my seat. I am taking my time, not rushing, and I note my body language is relaxed and positive. There is hopefully some laughter at my carefully chosen one-liners about the happy couple. This is the ideal outcome.

Right, so with this full target (a well-received speech) now crystallized in our mind, we move to the second phase – the brain is really brilliant at working out the process of *hitting the target* and we do this here by visualizing a cracking speech *in the first person*. In order to achieve this, in my film director's mind I come down from the bird's-eye view and imagine the scene all over again, but *this time through my own eyes.* I use incredibly fine detail and all my sensory perceptions to *experience exactly what I want to happen.* This is 'first-person visualization' and neuroscience backs it up heavily as being even more powerful because it uses your own senses and feelings to create an experience as if you were actually living it, moment by moment.

So, I imagine myself sitting at the top table at the reception. It's time to use ALL of my senses to really bring the movie to life, to BE the star of *Goodbye, Glossophobia.* I hear what I can hear – the clinking of glasses and lots of loud chattering. I see what I can see – all the guests in their finery, smiling and having a lovely time. I smell whatever smells are present – food, flowers, maybe perfume. I feel the floor beneath my feet and the posh chair I am resting on. I switch on my Zen Breathing right up to the point at which I rise from my seat . . . Show time!

I take my time, check with the back of the room that I can be heard, feel the cue cards in my hand . . . keep it short and hopefully sweet . . . I experience myself delivering a great speech – just the right length, just the right number of jokes before finishing off with an emotional tribute to the happy couple, followed by an enthusiastic round of applause.

Then I take my seat, relax, reach for a big swig of my cold beer and realize that I have completed my challenge. Everything has gone brilliantly. No Monkey Meltdown, no crises, no problems. Sounds like a perfect ending, and it is. Always remember, in your Hollywood Movie *you* are not only the star but also the writer, producer and director. No one else is telling you what to do next, or how to do it. That's why you can always visualize the perfect story.

What has this visualization done exactly? Well, it has programmed my brain to direct my body to follow the instructions for a successful, confident speech in particularly challenging circumstances. The brain is the Boss, the body must always follow. By using this process, you are dumbing down your conscious mind (the Monkey) and allowing the right hemisphere of your brain (where your imagination also resides) to dominate. If I have mentally rehearsed something properly, in fine detail, then when the time actually arrives to do it for real, I will actually feel as if I have succeeded in my challenge before I've even started!

The finest simulator in the world is not at the headquarters of any Formula One racing team, it is in your subconscious mind. The crucial element of this technique (backed up by hard neuroscience) is that when your subconscious does the mental rehearsal, *it does not know the difference between what you are imagining and the real thing.*

Just look at how you feel when you wake up suddenly from a scary nightmare – sweating, heart racing, anxious, frightened. Yet you are lying in a warm, safe bed. Your subconscious mind can't tell the difference. That illustrates how powerful this Tool can be. I am not surmising here – science can actually prove that when you are visualizing subconsciously, the same brain cells and maps you would use to actually carry out a 'skill' are fired up, and they are exactly the same cells as the ones that would be used to carry out that event in real life.

Regularly practising correct visualization techniques allows your confidence to blossom and continue to grow. This leads to improved performance and greater success, which in turn boosts your confidence even more. You will find yourself right in the centre of a circle of positivity and it feels great!

And it just gets better and better . . .

True confidence is self-perpetuating. Being increasingly and consistently confident brings more and more success, which in turn brings more confidence, and so on. You are effectively building a House of Self-belief. Every success allows you to add another floor, create another storey, until you maximize your full potential, achieve all your goals, live all your daydreams.

If your confidence continues to grow, you enter the realm of genuine self-belief. This is where all the great champions reside. Look around and you will find sports legends such as Muhammad Ali, Roger Federer, Serena Williams, Lewis Hamilton, Jessica Ennis-Hill; great leaders such as Winston Churchill, Margaret Thatcher, Nelson Mandela, Mahatma Gandhi, the Dalai Lama, Abraham Lincoln, Martin Luther King; mavericks and pioneers such as Florence Nightingale, Rosalind Franklin, Marie Curie and Amelia Earhart; and business moguls and entrepreneurs such as Jeff Bezos, Steve

Jobs, Sir Richard Branson, Henry Ford, Bill Gates, Elon Musk, Tim Berners-Lee, et al.

I would define self-belief as a strong feeling deep inside your soul that you can overcome whatever challenge lies in front of you, wherever. Self-belief also empowers you to know that when things don't go to plan, you can bounce back sooner rather than later. You know you can trust your skills to get you over the line and you back yourself to sort it out. 'Bouncebackability' is now a recognized word in the Oxford English Dictionary, and it lives in your House of Self-belief along with the paintings/drawings/photos of all your past wins and successes, on every wall of every storey.

Self-belief is not just for the sporting greats and the history-makers. It is yours to have and enjoy the benefits of every day. So use your Hollywood Movie Tool to prepare to be the best you can be in any given situation. If you practise and focus on each and every scene in your movie in tiny detail, then your confidence will be turbo-charged like never before.

Time to leave the cinema . . . Roll credits!

Case Study

Hollywood Movie
Martin

Mary, Martin's lovely partner, told me all about his medical issues and it appeared that the medical profession had all but given up on him. They told him he was physically well and therefore suggested it must be 'in his head'. As you will see, it was indeed 'in his head' but not in the way the doctors meant. Mary tells Martin's story of his recovery so beautifully, all I can add is that she and Martin did the work, not me. It is wonderful to know that to this day he is still enjoying all the things he did before his operation . . . especially that he succeeded in getting 'back on his bike'! Martin had lost confidence in his body's ability to heal, because of a significant mind/body disconnect. The main Tool used in his recovery is Hollywood Movie, a blockbuster starring Martin on his beloved motorbike . . .

Martin and I met late summer 2001. I made curtains for his sister and she asked me to deliver them to his house as she lived in London at that time. Late autumn I delivered another pair of curtains to the site where he was working. An afternoon walk and supper and here we are, eighteen years later.

Let me continue with a few bullet points from my notes on his illness and recovery:

- In 2001, I believe he discussed hearing loss and a problem with his balance with his doctor, which led on to an MRI scan.
- Martin found out he had a benign acoustic neuroma in May 2001.
- He was referred to a specialist consultant neurosurgeon that October and was given the choice to do nothing (not really an option) or have it removed. If left, the lump would continue to grow – it had already eaten away at Martin's hearing and may/would continue to damage other parts beyond the small ear canal and into the brain. Martin was put on the waiting list to have it removed.
- I remember dropping Martin off at hospital the day before his operation. He played hide-and-seek with me as he slowly made his way to Ward 3 and out of sight.
- I was not living with Martin at the time but I was very much in love with him. The thought of him

having eight hours of brain surgery the following day . . . I just wished it wasn't happening . . .

- Martin had his operation on the morning of 29 July 2002.

- I remember hiding in the car park at work while I waited until I could phone the hospital to ask whether he was out of surgery and if all was well.

- He looked quite comical in his hospital bed, with his turban-like head bandage and white surgical stockings on his long, slender legs. Over the course of my visits to the hospital, he was always hungry, wobbly on his legs but independent of mind. By that, I mean determined to help himself. He needed his routine, his physical and mental strength, and a return to normality as soon as possible. Some sort of inner 'unreason' (my word) did not want to give in to weakness.

- He stayed at his sister's for a short while after the operation until it was time to get back to a quiet routine.

- I think I moved in with Martin in spring 2003.

- 10 September 2002: Martin had a check-up with his consultant. Martin's notes say, 'Felt pretty good. Balance and orientation improving.'

- Some words about Martin's work ethic: 8 a.m. to 5.30 p.m. a day, in the dark, in the rain, those are his working hours. He does not accept help easily, likes to do stuff himself. If the job asks him to dig, Kango drill, lift heavy stuff, work around his feet and above his head, he just does it. Even though he knows it will hurt his sore head.

- Coming up to three months after the operation, from Martin's notes: 'Oct 21–5. Did some work for Tess [his sister] in Norfolk. No headaches but pretty tired after a full day's work. Generally pleased with the way I felt physically.'
- 'Nov. Few small jobs for friends; nothing too energetic.'
- 'Mid-November. Went to doctors. Quite painful sinus-type pain. Course of antibiotics. Useless.'
- 'End of Nov. Started getting headaches, but not too bad. Headaches getting progressively worse.'
- 'Dec 12. Went to doctors. Headaches getting worse. Referred to hospital.'
- 'Since then headaches have been pretty constant. Pills alleviate them but never quite disappear. Some extremely painful, especially in the morning or early hours. Take pills three or four times a day depending on severity. Balance has become affected. Comments from blokes at work (not known usually for their sympathetic

responses particularly) about a pained look in my eyes. Headaches now wearing me down. Very tired.'

- No more Martin notes after this point.
- Another appointment with the consultant on 11 February 2003.
- I think Martin needed a different approach to his post-surgery headaches/persisting-headache syndrome. On 1 July 2003 he saw a different doctor.
- Over this period he started taking a combination of painkillers and anti-depressants. He was sleeping badly, rolling his head and moving around the bed. He would be cradling his head, looking for a position where it did not hurt. Most noticeable was his weight loss. The pain was eating into his physical condition, wasting his muscle and strength. His balance was unpredictable. He was really struggling.
- Martin carried on working throughout this time. Better to keep busy as the alternative was uninterrupted pain. He did not want any fuss or interference and would refuse help. Luckily he was mostly working for/with people that cared for and looked out for him.
- Martin passed out at work one morning (a good few weeks before I first phoned Don). His 6 feet

2 inches fell like a tree in all the dust and rubble of a building site. Mike, the chap he was working with, phoned me – he knew Martin would not want an ambulance. I took him home where he was completely disorientated and just slept. He did end up in hospital later that day for tests because he had been unconscious for so long. All was good.

- He did say to me, 'Is this it?'

- After this point, I just had to do something. I was quietly doing stuff around him/for him/behind his back that took away any worry and pressure. Trying to eliminate the really hard stuff. Talking to his friends, the guys he was working with, doing whatever I could to enable his body to heal. He was annoyed with me when he did find out some of the stuff I was doing . . . but what can you do? He was not really helping himself. He just carried on doing what he knows. Awful thing to watch.

- My dad died from cancer very young – fifty-two. He had so much life in him. Dad used self-hypnosis – he needed help with the stuff that was going on within himself and around him. It's quite a helpless feeling – his cancer was just going to do its thing. There was no stopping it. I used to do the sessions with him. And they did help.

- With my dad's experience in mind, using the Yellow Pages and the library I collected four names. I phoned the first three – all men (not many women around then). My idea was to try to engage with these men/professionals over the phone, to see if they communicated/ connected with me and understood Martin's position at that moment. I knew Martin would not tolerate a weak character who sounded like he was reading out of a textbook – hypnotherapy/psychology by numbers – which was exactly how the first three men sounded.

- You, Don, were different. You listened, your voice was strong without being bullying, and you did not try to push your ideas on me. You sounded as though you would be able to adjust your practice to suit an individual's personality and needs. I felt you understood.

- For that first meeting Martin cycled over to you in pain, and after your time together he cycled along the canal light-headed with a quiet mind. You uncluttered the pain for a short while in that first session, and over the eight that followed you worked together with Martin to teach him how to understand his body and take control. Most important of all, Don, you connected with Martin and he believed in you.

It was clever of you to zoom in on his motorbike passion.

- He was so sceptical of this form of treatment, and under normal circumstances would not have given it the time of day. There was nowhere else for him to go, though – the doctors, consultants, painkillers and anti-depressants weren't working. In fact, the combination of pills Martin was taking was just making the pain worse. The pills were having their own private battle with each other, creating their own brand of pain. When combined with Martin's original post-op pain it resulted in a destructive force. It needed some unravelling, and over the course of a year you worked wonders.

- Martin is seventy-two this year. Still playing squash. Still riding his motorbike and cycling. He works four days a week. Well, that is the aim but it doesn't always happen. He still has low-level headaches and a few wobbles, which he can manage if he is sensible (not all the time). Truth is, he would not know what to do with himself if he stopped working. Still sticking to the routine that's important to him. A few aches and pains, but he is essentially as fit as a flea.

Fairly soon into our early sessions, Martin made it clear he was determined to enjoy his life and to reconnect as soon as possible to the happier, pain-free days. In particular he wanted to re-engage his passion for riding his motorbike. So, we continued to use the Zen Breathing Tool and the Kaizen until he could gradually relax his body himself, especially the muscles in his scalp, neck and shoulders, and therefore be more able to adjust and reduce the headaches progressively to a much more manageable level.

When I recorded a personal mp3 for him, we were able to include strong visualizations of being back on his bike. I asked him to hear the roar of the engine, sense the air rushing by, feel the tyres biting into the surface of the road and the handlebars in his grip through his gloves. I asked him to feel the acceleration and the braking, the motion and dynamics of the bike as it danced beneath him, fully connected, harmoniously in sync . . . and once again riding freely and able to enjoy all the joy it brought him. This was Martin's Hollywood Movie, and he was most certainly the star.

Tool 5

Get Out of Your Head

How to Concentrate and
On-demand Focus

'Concentrate!' is an instruction most of us will have been on the receiving end of at one time or another. Kids, more often than not, have this word shouted at them! But have you ever asked yourself, what exactly *is* concentration? One definition is 'the deliberate act, or process, of directing ALL of your attention on to one particular object, or task'. I believe concentration is also an art and a vital life skill that some people are much better at than others. Your ability to concentrate will directly affect many areas of your life, so it is important that you learn how to perform this crucial skill.

Plenty of examples of incredible concentration skills in action exist all around us. Let's start with one of our beloved family pets: I often used to watch our cat George from my office window as he waited patiently for a mouse to reappear from behind a bush. He was as still as a statue (no doubt

Zen Breathing), his soft eyes gazing with laser-beam focus on the bush. George had clearly mastered the art of focused control, his mind and body fully connected but totally relaxed. When he finally pounced, he would do so instinctively and decisively, not thinking, just highly focused 'doing'. There would only ever be one outcome. For the benefit of mouse-lovers and those of a sensitive disposition, I will say no more . . .

Humans can master this art, too. When I watch sports professionals in action, I can easily see which players have the most 'relaxed' concentration. And you don't need to be an expert to watch a tennis match where one player is serene and focused while the other has a meltdown, in order to guess whose concentration is better?

I work with many famous snooker players, and that is a sport requiring immense powers of concentration. Those who emerge as champions are the ones who are able to clip a ball some twelve feet away with pin-point accuracy in the final frame of a big tournament, in front of hundreds or sometimes thousands of people (all of whom are sitting in silence in the auditorium), knowing that millions of people are also watching at home. Generally speaking, the top level of sport is populated with people who have honed their powers of concentration to perfection because, quite simply, no one can get to the top without such focus.

In the entertainment business, too, I see people with incredible powers of concentration. The professionals on *Strictly Come Dancing*, for instance, are so engrossed in the present moment – using all of their physical prowess, coordination and muscle memory, their skills and senses – that they become one with the performance: the dancer becomes the dance.

It's not just elite, high-profile individuals who can concentrate with such precision, though. Take the wonderful people in our armed forces. They might, for example, be on patrol in a dangerous country, walking along a deserted road, surrounded by buildings, potential hidden risks at every turn. Yet they have to read their environment in a split-second, be mindful of their mission and the movements and position of their colleagues around them, and then, if an extreme incident occurs, focus their concentration even more sharply in order to stay alive. At least in sport, if you let your concentration slip, you lose a game or a point, or maybe even a tournament. If a soldier drifts off and loses focus . . . well, they might pay the ultimate price.

This demonstrates how humans can immediately access 'on-demand', full-on focus when they find themselves in a dangerous situation. Other examples might be engaging in a risky activity such as rock climbing; performing surgery; or reacting to a sudden, unexpected event on the road. People in these circumstances are able to give their total focus to the task in hand because it might be a life-or-death situation; every ounce of mental concentration simply has to be on the task for every single moment until the challenge, and the actual threat to their safety (or that of others), is over.

Of course, there are plenty of examples of concentration in everyday life: think of a teenager going for a personal best on a computer game, a kid opening a Christmas present, a dog with a juicy bone . . . The list is endless.

What is usually more evident in everyday life is a *lack* of concentration. You might encounter it when driving on the motorway, for example – you might see a car drifting across lanes. I recently saw someone walk into a lamp post because they were looking at their phone rather than concentrating on where they were walking. I'm sure we're all guilty of drifting off in a meeting (or during a class), only to find out later that we've missed out on important information.

When your mind and body are in complete harmony, concentration happens naturally without you having to think about it; when there is a mind–body disconnect for any reason, things can go very wrong, very quickly.

Eastern martial arts experts have known for hundreds of years that higher levels of concentration are the key to opening the box of better performance. To quote Rod Laver, one of the greatest tennis players of all time, 'In concentration you have to wipe everything out of your mind except the ball. Nothing but the ball. Glue your eyes to it. Marry it! Don't let it out of your sight. Make that ball an obsession. If you get yourself into that trance, pressure won't intrude. It's just you and the ball.'

You might read all of this and think, *I will never be a tennis champion or a soldier on patrol, so how does this apply to me?* Well, how to concentrate is possibly the single most important Tool I can teach you. The art of relaxed concentration is a solid foundation for being calm, at ease and confident: effortless effort. We all have this capacity. Whether it is an act, a science, an art (or all three), one thing is for sure, concentration is the boss of all mental skills, the Zen of all mental mastery, because without it nothing can be achieved. The good news is that anyone, anywhere and at any time is capable of learning how to improve their concentration.

During my work with tennis players, the most common sound I hear coming from the courts isn't that of the ball leaving the strings of a racket, it is the coaches bellowing 'Concentrate!' at their (often flustered) protégés. Good advice, in theory, but I always wonder if anyone has ever taught these talented kids *how* to concentrate? And then how to take that focus and skill to a higher level? In order to teach you how to concentrate better (and help change your life), I first need to explain what is happening when your concentration is poor.

It's time to Get Out of Your Head.

Let's start by testing your existing powers of concentration so we have a baseline to work from.

Grab a pencil and hold it in your hand. Now, turn all your attention to that pencil, cut out any distractions and simply focus on the item in your hand. I want you to become really *engrossed* in the pencil: fascinated and focused. Switch on all your sensory perceptions as you examine it. Feel its shape, connect to it, love it! Does it feel smooth to the touch? What colour is it? Can you smell the wood? Does it have an eraser at one end and a nice sharp point at the other?

If you can do this, then you are starting to concentrate. The longer you stay connected with all your senses, the more you become 'locked in' to the pencil and turbo-charge your powers of concentration.

Another popular version of this technique is to look into the flame of a candle. The brightness of the light and the seductive dance of the flame can be incredibly relaxing to watch – almost trance-like – because your eye muscles will tire after a few minutes, in the same way they would if a stage hypnotist asked you to look up at the bright lights above the stage, or at a swinging watch, perhaps. It is applying the same principle, so pencil or flame, give it a go!

I will wager, however, that on your first few attempts, it won't be long before you start to drift off. It is always more difficult to stay focused on a dull and uninteresting task – but far more beneficial and rewarding concentration practice.

What actually happens when you lose your focus is one of two things sabotages your concentration: external distractions or your Monkey. In many cases, you can take action to eliminate external distractions (turn off the radio, make sure you're in a quiet room, and so on). In other cases, those distractions might be out of your control – when you're making a presentation in a busy room, for example – and it is how you react to those distractions that will affect your concentration.

Someone or something distracting you, either deliberately or accidentally, is obviously annoying and off-putting. I would suggest one of two strategies to deal with this:

1) immerse yourself even more into the process of what you are doing, increase your sensory perceptions and simply block out the distractions; 2) switch on your Zen Breathing and stay 'locked in' to it, thereby remaining in control of your Monkey and, in turn, your emotions and motor skills.

The second concentration saboteur is internal Monkey Chatter, and this *is* within your control. Pretty soon after you pick up the pencil, your Monkey might say, 'This is boring! It's just a pencil!' And to some degree the Monkey is right, it is just a pencil, but that's not the point. To be fully focused on the 'doing', you must be in the 'now', and unfortunately the Monkey is rubbish at being in the now – it loves being in the past or in the 'what if' future. With all that chatter going on in your head, it's often impossible to concentrate properly, if at all.

If you want to achieve the purest form of focus of all – the Art of Relaxed Concentration – the Monkey must be managed. Pure concentration means being able to keep the Monkey Mind firmly in the present moment, anchored to the here and now. The Monkey, of course, lives in your head, and that is why this particular brain-tuning Tool is called Get Out of Your Head.

I want you to imagine stepping into a lift in your head and going down into your body. When my Monkey (Mike) is particularly stroppy and intrusive (as he sometimes is), I visualize getting into the lift in my head and watching myself press the button marked 'basement'. The button illuminates as I press it and I hear the doors close softly. A voice (not Mike) says, 'Going down,' and is followed by a *ping*. Within seconds the doors open silently and I am now safely cocooned in the middle of my body, where all I can hear is the gentle sound of my Zen Breathing, reminding me of waves lapping on the seashore – in and out, such a soothing, comforting rhythm. Very quickly I am no longer able to hear Mike the Monkey . . . No more Monkey Chatter.

At this stage I take myself on a guided tour of my body. You can start to do this by visualizing your right thumb, then picture each finger on that hand in turn, moving on to your palm, the back of your hand. Go on to your arms, shoulders, legs and so on, travelling around your body in great detail for as long as you like, but even a few minutes will be enough to establish a strong mind–body connection. Your Monkey Chatter will have ceased and you will successfully have been able to Get Out of Your Head.

There are other simple techniques to help you get out of your head and improve your concentration. One popular and effective method is to focus all your attention on your breath, but not the Zen Breathing we've learned about, which is *breath control*. This time you need to switch to *breath awareness*.

Find a quiet spot and follow your breath as you inhale all the way in through your nose, then follow it all the way out as you exhale through your nose (or your mouth, if you prefer). Do not make any attempt to control your breath – let it do its own thing, at any speed or rhythm. Simply observe it and stay with it for as long as you can. Your breath will always anchor you immediately to the now, and by doing so will automatically generate on-demand concentration in that exact moment.

Just like with the pencil task, do not be alarmed if it's not long before you hear your Monkey saying, 'This is soooooo boring!' This is not an easy exercise, but remember, the more difficult the practice, the stronger your powers of concentration will be! So persevere, and practise these skills. Once you feel able to glide into your own personal lift and get out of your head with relative ease, or to switch on your breath awareness, you are ready to start applying these skills to the aspects of your everyday life that need this new, focused concentration.

Nobody can concentrate 100 per cent of the time – it simply isn't possible – but many of us need to concentrate a lot of the time. There are moments when higher levels of concentration are needed immediately, such as when giving a big speech, delivering an important presentation, driving a car on a busy road, performing an operation in hospital . . . When you *really* need to focus, these techniques will enable you to switch on your on-demand concentration for perfect results.

Best performance = talent/skill – distractions

Whenever you see someone focusing intently on a particular task or object in everyday life, their eyes will be soft and relaxed as opposed to staring and tense. Consequently, their muscles will also be relaxed – ready for calm, composed action rather than tensed for impulsive moves. Pure concentration doesn't mean staring hard at something or looking intense, it's more about finding ways of keeping your conscious Monkey Mind interested so it cannot interfere with your skills, and prevent you performing at your best.

The exercises in this chapter will help you strengthen your powers of concentration so that you will soon be able to switch them on with extreme focus. Keep practising these techniques regularly – ideally every day, even for just a few minutes. Of course, there will still be moments in your life when an unexpected or high-pressure situation pops up and you will need to manually tap into your 'reserve tank' of instant concentration. However, if you have done these exercises, those extreme moments will be far more easily managed. For the more mundane moments when you need to focus on a task or object, you will quickly start to feel far more capable of staying 'out of your head' and on target.

Remember, concentration (being in the now) is a very challenging skill to master; being in the present moment is pure, undiluted concentration. Learning to access on-demand concentration – and, crucially, staying there long enough to achieve the best performance – is the most difficult mental skill but also the most important one.

So, go on, jump in that lift and press the button . . .

Case Study

Get Out of Your Head

Dr Raj – Scalpel Meets the Monkey!

I met Dr Raj Jutley when we were both working with young racers. He himself was a very fine, enthusiastic rally driver. Oh yes, and by the way, he is also one of the most eminent and skilful cardiac surgeons in the world! Raj and I became good friends, and remain so to this day. Heart surgeons are the Red Arrows of the medical profession (he told me!), although I guess neurosurgeons might have something to say about that.

Raj always works under extreme pressure during heart-bypass operations and asked if I could help him to remain calm and focused, and also to help teach his operating team to stay totally focused when the pressure is on in theatre. As you might expect, Zen Breathing featured heavily, as well as Mind the Monkey, but the main Tool in Raj's story was Get Out of Your Head. Failure in theatre was never an option, so getting out of his head and instantly connecting to his body – especially his hands – blocked any interference from the Monkey at the most crucial times!

To be perfectly honest, I really didn't believe in the 'mumbo-jumbo' of the Monkey Mind before I met Don. I soon discovered that even without me knowing about it, I was in fact practising taming my Monkey Mind – the constantly chattering, restless, largely unhelpful Monkey that would sit on my shoulder before any surgery and comment incessantly about the operation and what could go wrong with it. I realize now that this is in fact a defence mechanism of sorts, which protects humans, but at the same time, for those who work in high-stress environments it might actually make the difference between success and failure, particularly if your concentration is badly affected.

When I got to Don's, he explained our session would be short and involve him entering my head, so off we went. I sat in a comfortable armchair with my shoes off. There was background music playing. I recall thinking, *What the f**k is this guy going to do without a scalpel?* Within a few minutes (I still cannot understand how), Don was in my head, explaining to me about breathing, visualization and, of course, the Monkey.

How did I feel? Certainly very cautious, and even apprehensive initially, but not long after, I was extremely relaxed – to the point that I actually fell asleep. Gone was the tension at the back of my head, the muscles in my scalp actually relaxed, and I could feel my forehead wrinkles soften. Don used visualization techniques focusing on childhood memories to trigger and deepen the session and, of course, his baritone voice was the perfect complement to what he was saying.

I consider that day a significant one in my life. A day when I embraced the importance of the mind in optimizing performance – poor concentration in my profession can have very serious consequences. Don and I spoke about my Monkey Mind and decided that the next time I was going into surgery and had to spend the mandatory five to eight minutes scrubbing my hands before gowning up, I would in fact talk to my Monkey and ask it to stay in the scrub room while I performed the operation. I learned to use the tactile nature of both hands touching as the catalyst for the taming. Now, if a case is especially challenging and critical – such as a torn aorta that has been blue-lighted to me in the middle of the night – I can tell my Monkey to sleep but be on standby when I need it. I have an understanding with my fellow primate! My concentration and level of precise focus have improved significantly.

One would think that surgeons receive this type of training as par for the course. Well, I certainly did not, and it is only relatively recently that the Royal Colleges are recognizing the importance of human factors in surgical outcomes and performance.

Taming the Monkey Mind is not easy. Humans are hard-wired to ensure survival, so there will always be a Monkey – large or small, loud or quiet – sitting on everyone's shoulder, chattering away and commenting on each move, thought or action. That Monkey is there to make sure we don't overdo it to the point of self-harm. That Monkey Mind needs to be synchronized with what you are aiming to achieve at that moment so that you can concentrate and hit your maximum performance, and it also needs to be parked somewhere safe and close by to be called upon immediately if and when required. Thanks to Don I have also managed to get the Monkey to congratulate me when the outcomes have been good. Hell, sometimes the Monkey even speaks to me in Don's accent! Now isn't that a great measure of success!

Tool 6

Feathering the Brakes

How to Introduce More Control into Your Life

Do you sometimes feel as if you are in the fast lane of a motorway and can't switch to a slower lane? Do you experience feelings of being overwhelmed, rushed or out of control, even? Life is so fast these days, and in the modern age there are so many accelerators that relentlessly increase the tempo, such as the internet, social media, television, career demands, and so on.

Speed has become a way of life – faster broadband, faster deliveries, fast food, fast fashion, faster cars, speed dating . . . I certainly sense the pace of my life has accelerated significantly during the last few years – the weeks and months fly by, blurring into years, and years into decades. I sometimes feel that I am a passenger on a runaway train without a driver. Time flies indeed – in fact, I might have the Latin – *tempus fugit* – etched on to my gravestone, as nothing else feels more appropriate.

This way of life can be exciting if you enjoy tapping into that energy and have the Tools to cope when life becomes too rapid – but if you find that relentless urgency over-whelming and a constant challenge, then you can be left feeling as if you have no sense of control over your life. And with that lack of feeling of being in control comes an in-evitable increase in anxiety . . .

We need some context here – of course, life has always been stressful to one degree or another. Anyone who lived through the Second World War would certainly have had plenty of anxiety to deal with, and they might also feel somewhat perplexed when they overhear that it is 'a total disaster' that someone has lost followers on Instagram. However, modern life has its own challenges – it is undoubt-edly much faster in so many ways than in years gone by, and it seems at times that there are just too many elements all vying for our attention.

Part of the challenge is that although modern life may be more full on than a hundred, or even fifty years ago, our brains have not adapted. There simply hasn't been enough time for the human brain to evolve physically to cope with these increased demands. Indeed, can our brains cope at this current speed of life? Is our brain designed to go this fast?

The answer is that, yes, you can train yourself to cope with the rapidity of modern life. The brain is the most remarkable piece of equipment: look at how a racing driver is able to train their brain to process the huge amount of information that hurtles at them at great speed on every single lap for two hours of a race. Of course it takes years of training for the drivers to develop the ability on this scale, but the good news is that you too can train your brain to manage a rapid receipt of information – and it won't take you years to learn how!

First, let me remind you of the simple but critical truth that YOU are in control. This is because you ARE the brain. The body only does what its brain tells it. You have the ability to be in control of the speed at which your brain is running. I'd like to make this point in more detail by using a very simple analogy: comparing our brain to a car engine. In reality our brains are far more sophisticated, smarter, faster and more reliable than any engine, but the parallels between the two allow me to highlight how to deal with a faster pace of life in very simple ways.

Just like your car's engine, if you go too fast for too long, keeping your foot down hard on the accelerator, you are going to use far more fuel. Just as your car's engine can become flooded, your brain too can become soaked in adrenalin, and at that point the ability to remain calm and not feel anxious becomes much more challenging. If you keep on travelling at high speed you may well start to damage your engine. Certain components might overheat and you could run out of fuel. You might even break down altogether.

As with any engine, if you don't treat the wonderful piece

of kit that is your brain with some TLC, there could be damaging consequences. After all, you take your car for an MOT and a service, so why wouldn't you look after your brain? Modern society talks a lot about looking after our physical health – exercise classes, healthy diets, detoxes . . . Yet taking care of our brain seems to come way down that list of priorities.

If you indulge me in continuing with the metaphor of the brain being an engine, there are some useful parallels to help you gain and maintain good mental health. Neuroscientists tell us that the brain basically has four 'speeds' (cycles per second): Delta, Theta, Alpha and Beta, measured in Hertz (Hz, named after the German physicist Heinrich Hertz, 1857–94). The number of Hz equals the number of cycles per second, so the lower the Hz, the slower your brain is working. In my analogy, our brains effectively have a four-speed gearbox:

First gear: Delta = 1–4 Hz
Second gear: Theta = 4–8 Hz
Third gear: Alpha = 8–14 Hz
Fourth gear: Beta = 14–40 Hz

A balanced, healthy brain needs all the 'gears' working seamlessly in order to function efficiently. For example:

- To concentrate, you need your brain in fourth gear (Beta);

- For relaxation, calm or meditation, select third gear (Alpha);
- For sleep with dreams and deeper relaxation, it's second gear (Theta);
- And for deeper sleep without dreams, it's first gear (Delta).

During an average day and night, you are changing gear constantly, without being aware of which gear you are in at any given time. In other words, your gearbox is in 'automatic' mode, which is fine if all is going well. However, if your brain somehow ends up in the wrong gear at the wrong time, because your life is too frenetic and too complicated, then you will encounter problems. The side effects of being stuck in too high a gear for too long are likely to be stress, depression, anxiety, poor sleep quality and so on.

Out on the road, one way of slowing down a car travelling at too high a speed – with or without using the brakes – is to change down from fourth gear to third, and so on. It's something you would have to do manually and fairly quickly. The exact same principle applies to your over-revving brain. But how can we change our own gears manually and slow down our brains?

By using my next Tool: Feathering the Brakes.

What do I mean by this? Let me explain by way of a few examples of how people live their lives at speed: driving in a rush, often for no reason; eating too quickly, in order to move on to the next task at hand; talking too fast, or talking at someone and not actually listening to their reply; rushing about so much that moments you should really enjoy, such as spending time with your kids or looking after yourself, fall by the wayside. The constant search for 'bigger, better, faster' in our society exacerbates this sense of a fast-paced existence. It is often far more rewarding to slow down – perhaps even stop sometimes – and appreciate what you already have.

Often, we become habitualized in certain ways of life and, in extreme cases, these can become addictions. Those such as gambling, alcohol and drugs are indeed serious challenges. However, are we even more addicted to thinking? To Monkey Chatter? Are too many of us living in the Land of What If?

Unfortunately the Monkey is rubbish at being in the present, and the pace of modern life means it is all too easy for it to constantly entice you into the past, or even the future. But if you are not here, not in the now, then you are not really living. You are enduring rather than enjoying! Maybe you can think of something you do without actually doing it? Especially something you really should enjoy and engage with.

I love taking my Labrador, Penny, for walks along the canal towpath, surrounded by beautiful scenery. But I am not really walking. I catch myself thinking as the Monkey chatters away, distracting me from the joys of the walk, reminding me to send an email or to check the car's tax is not out of date. I have to bring myself back to the walk constantly, by raising my sensory perceptions – hearing and feeling my feet along the gravel of the path, seeing and hearing the trees sway gently in the breeze, feeling the warm air on my skin, watching Penny rummaging in the grass and bushes for something to eat, dodging a Lycra-clad cyclist as they rush past me silently! Unfortunately, some people become so wrapped up in their constant thinking and rushed way of life – without realizing it – that sadly they go right through their lives without actually living.

Whenever we feel stressed or anxious there is a strong tendency to move more quickly – to walk and talk faster. If you aren't mindful of this and your speed continues unchecked, you could end up like a racing driver who goes into a corner too fast, loses traction, leaves the track and, as ex-F1 driver and commentator Martin Brundle would say, heads 'straight to the scene of the accident'. In this scenario, you would be in big trouble if you were to just slam on the brakes. The forces acting on your car and body would be too great, you would struggle to maintain control, and there would be a high chance of a catastrophic incident.

Instead, you have to learn to do what all great racing drivers do when they realize that they are going too fast: they feather their brakes. In racing, this means softly and gently scrubbing some speed out of the car – not stopping or lurching to a slower speed – but touching the brakes gently so that the car slows to a speed that is more manageable, appropriate and, most importantly, *under control*. You can learn to slow down your thoughts, too, by Feathering the Brakes of your Monkey Chatter.

First up, have a good, honest look at your life. We humans often have a tendency to make things in our lives more complicated than they need to be. It pours petrol on to the fire and wastes valuable brain resources. One very effective way of slowing down and feathering your brakes is to *simplify* as much as you can in your life.

Are you taking on too much?

Are you looking to please people all the time?

Do you find it difficult to say no?

Do you have commitments that have become a burden rather than an enjoyable experience, but you continue with them for fear of letting down others?

Only you know the specifics of your daily life and routine, but what are you doing that you really *don't* have to? Maybe you could sit down and have a meeting with yourself: be honest and, crucially, *be kind to yourself.*

It's not just the specifics of your daily life that you can assess and pare back. What is going on in your brain can also be simplified. Certain neuroscientists have come up with the notion of 'decision-making fatigue'. Apparently, we make more than thirty thousand decisions every day, from what to wear when we get up, to what not to wear when we go to bed, and everything in between. Is this why Simon Cowell seems always to be wearing the same white shirts?

Jokes aside, all these decisions take up brain power and there's only a finite amount of that on tap – at some point, you will run dry. Just like a muscle you ask too much of during a gym session, your brain will lose power. After a long day of making thousands of decisions on your behalf, the brain can become so exhausted that it malfunctions to the point of making impulse decisions. This might be acting on a whim – without much thought or consideration as to the consequences – or simply packing up altogether and making no decisions at all. It's probably why, after a long, hard day at work, when my wife, Jane, asks me what I would like for supper, I'll often reply, 'I really don't mind – I'll leave it to you'. A tired brain that is asked too many questions can easily end up making a bad decision.

Being aware that you might be overdoing certain elements of your life will help you to reduce the volume of your daily decision-making. In turn, this will help to rest your brain. It is a very direct correlation: if your life is simpler, then the demands on your brain are lowered, too.

Making your life simpler is behind what has made so-called mindfulness so popular in recent times, although I must confess to being unsure of the term mind-*full*-ness – I would rather have the means to empty my mind rather than fill it! However, I haven't come up with an alternative, so it will have to do (mind-*empty*-ness doesn't quite cut the mustard, does it?). The point is, mindfulness – and indeed any form of meditation – is an excellent way of Feathering the Brakes and slowing down your Monkey Chatter, especially if slow Zen Breaths are involved too (see Tool 1 – page 31).

Another way of slowing things down is to train yourself

to be more childlike. Seeing life through the eyes of a child can help to simplify the things that, as adults, we tend to over-complicate. Kids are great at being in the now, aren't they? They seem to instinctively remove or ignore what isn't necessary, so they can see what they perceive to be important to them at any given moment. So, release your inner child. Keep it simple, don't waste the brain juice, and you will discover that simplicity is the absolute sweet spot between too much and too little. I believe there is real power and beauty in simplicity – I love it.

You can also help to Feather the Brakes by being aware of the physicality of your daily movements. Every now and then, pause and check whether you are moving too fast. I know that life is full and complicated, so it isn't always possible to go slowly. You might be at the supermarket, rushing about, knowing you have to get back to the school gates in time to pick up the kids . . . What then? That's fair enough – but what you can do is *slow down*. You can still calm yourself and your movements without missing the school pick-up, and you can breathe more slowly in the queue while you are waiting. This might not be the optimum breathing technique but can be a good temporary solution when you are out and about. What it will do is curb the Monkey Mind's excesses in that moment.

I've experienced some particularly challenging situations myself and I know how difficult things can be, but I am strongly urging you to make every attempt in stressful situations to *just slow down*. Buy yourself some time until you can get to a place where you can take more focused action with the other Tools in this book. Having regained control and slowed down to the point at which you are moving at a more leisurely and appropriate speed, you can then utilize your preferred Tools to get a hold on the situation in a calm and measured manner.

Here are some summary ideas on how to regain control and Feather Your Brakes.

1. Check your speed. Does it feel as if you are moving too fast?
2. Having checked your speed, move forward but take your time. Do you *really* need to rush?
3. Attend to your breathing. Tell it to slow down – deeper, slower . . .
4. Sit down if you can, then keep still – very still – for just a few minutes. Do this every day. Close your eyes (if safe to do so) and switch on the Zen Breathing Tool.
5. Let thoughts come, then let them go.
6. No more decision-making today, wherever possible.

Feathering the Brakes and thereby slowing down the Monkey Chatter has far greater benefits than just looking after your brain: a balanced mind also keeps your heart healthy, and boosts your immune, endocrine and digestive systems. Your brain works closely with all these vital body functions. In fact, neuroscience confirms that there are hundreds of neuron receptors in your heart that are connected to/communicating with your brain. The heart sends more messages to the brain than the brain sends back, which is another good reason to look after your brain so it can interpret the heart's messages accurately.

Your gut and digestive system talk to your brain in a similar way, and vice versa. Imagine your favourite meal in front of you now – you can't wait to get stuck in! But if you were to receive some news suddenly – an alarming or upsetting text message – then you will find that your appetite disappears almost immediately. This extreme change comes from a mere thought, a message from the brain to the stomach . . . Yet if you receive another text just as quickly, saying, 'Ignore the previous message, it was all a mistake,' then your appetite will miraculously return in a nanosecond as your brain sends an updated message to your gut that all is well, crack on, tuck in.

If you Feather the Brakes, you will have time to pause and reflect on the fact that at least 95 per cent of the things worrying you will, in reality, probably never happen. A friend of mine once told me that they had spent the last twenty years worrying about thousands of problems that never occurred. Does that sound familiar?

Simplifying your life, being more childlike and slowing yourself down across all areas of your life will reap major dividends. Even ten minutes of practising some of the techniques in this chapter will bring you wonderful calm and clarity. Nothing rushed was ever done well . . . so Feather the Brakes.

Trust me – your brain will thank you.

Case Study

Feathering the Brakes

Rob

In my experience, it seems that creative, hard-working, sensitive and caring people are more prone to ongoing anxiety, often resulting in depression. I suppose you could call this 'burnout'. Rob did, and probably still does, fit this category and he certainly is creative. Without realizing it, his life was speeding up significantly, and his overworked brain was using far too much energy, becoming more and more tired, eventually leaving him depressed.

The problem was that, like all creative people, Rob did not stop, although he most certainly needed to slow down. The key word that Rob had to come to understand and exercise was 'patience'. When depression has a tight hold and you are totally exhausted, physically and mentally, it is very hard to be patient. You want to feel 'normal' again . . . NOW. The most significant Tool used in helping Rob back to his own 'normality' was Feathering the Brakes – he can tell you how far better than I can.

As I'm writing this, I'm on my lunch break from my work as a freelance video editor. I'm a bit stressed about a couple of ambitious projects I've undertaken, but nothing out of the ordinary. I edited a video project and managed its release from my own company. It is the latest in a series of projects I've handled the creative and business release of over the last year. I have felt like my old self again, and have become more and more confident with each passing month. When I meet friends I haven't seen in a while, they comment on the difference.

At the end of 2016, I was in the midst of a nervous breakdown. I was on anti-depressants, and most days I couldn't get out of bed. For months, I would cry on a daily basis. My lifestyle – terrible diet, no exercise and coping with alcohol – was keeping me in the pits. I had ambitious, creative ideas that I couldn't even begin to execute because my mind was in such a state. I had just graduated from university and the real world hit me like a ton of bricks – as it does so many – and I just fell apart. After years of striving so hard whilst studying, I struggled to understand why I didn't have the next stage of my life figured out.

I was noticeably depressed. One day a friend of mine, who's an elite sports player, commented on it and put me in touch with Don. At the end of 2016,

I had a single session with Don, which lasted around two hours. He calmed me down first and explained that everything was going to be all right. He had complete confidence. I didn't at the time, but I put my faith in him. During the session, Don explained the concept of the Monkey Mind and asked me to tell him about my situation. He also explained the concept of Feathering the Brakes and how that would help me to slow down my life. He recommended some reading and also suggested tapering off the anti-depressants very gradually, under the guidance of my GP, Dr Julian Widdowson.

He then reassured me that he had complete faith that we could work together to get me back to full mental fitness, and he clarified one important point – I would need to have patience. To go from a nervous breakdown to peak mental performance is not something that happens overnight, and it would require my faith that together we would get there.

Over the next few months I experienced a 'two steps forward, one step back' journey of recovery, that turned into 'five steps forward, one step back'. Setbacks from which it would have taken me weeks to recover previously were overcome in one week, then a few days, then a single day.

After just over a year, I took my last anti-depressant at the end of 2017. By then I was initiating creative projects and working full time. I was enjoying the journey, going with the flow and not taking life too seriously – all the while achieving everything I'd set out to accomplish when I first went to see Don. My vitality had returned. This growth continued into the next year until the point I am at now – one of quiet confidence and determination.

Don wasn't a therapist or a counsellor, his methods and recommendations empowered me to re-programme my mind. I learned that I was in control and I could manage the Monkey Mind myself. From this I was able to recover, leave the 'survive' stage and begin to 'thrive'. Essentially, I took back control of my life. Don enabled me to re-train my mind to engineer my own recovery, and Feathering the Brakes played a big part in that turnaround.

I still have a lot of personal development to do. I have bad days, but I ride them out and see life for what it is. There are moments of frustration, procrastination and feeling low, but the virtuous cycle of strong positive habits I've built have been reducing these moments day by day. I was really bad when I met Don. In many ways, Don has helped me to achieve the ultimate 'success' in life – I'm finally able to say, 'I'm doing good, cheers,' and mean it.

Tool 7

Neurobics

How to Generate More Brain Power

Every year, when 1 January arrives, many of us declare New Year's resolutions – some of which are more ambitious than others. Drink less, spend less, learn a foreign language, finally pass a driving test, start walking regularly (although my wife says I already ramble a lot) . . .

There are thousands of common resolutions, but perhaps the single most popular 'promise to the self' is to get fit. New gym membership numbers always spike massively in January, then inevitably tail off in February and start to get cancelled by many people before spring has even arrived. I want to highlight society's focus on the body and physical fitness here, because how many people do you speak to in the first week of the New Year who tell you that their resolution is 'to get my brain in better shape'?

I'd wager not many!

These days we are over-trained physically but under-trained mentally. Modern society has continually insisted that in order to be happy and healthy, we must look after our body, and of course being fit physically is indeed vitally important. But without good mental health to complement our physical wellbeing, we may be storing up all sorts of problems, no matter how impressive our six pack is or how far we can run. It is a simple fact that if the brain doesn't function well, the body cannot possibly be at its best, or healthiest. If we can agree that our brains are at least as important as our bodies, how come we hear so much more about the importance of physical exercise, healthy eating, other physical lifestyle choices, yet so little about mental exercise and brain workouts? Although it is fair to add that conversation about mental health has opened up significantly in the last few years, the emphasis still seems to be more focused on the body than the brain.

In sport, as in life, we should be seeking a healthy balance between mind and body in order to feel, and be, at our best. We should actively take better care of our brain, so that it can continue to look after our body as we grow older. Thanks to the wonders of modern science and a greater understanding of the ageing process, we are all living longer. Aside from obvious exceptions where disease or more challenging living conditions prevail, the World Health Organization (WHO) states that between 2000 and 2016 alone, life expectancy rose an average of 5.5 years.

Part of the current imbalance in the emphasis on physical and mental exercise in society is down to the fact that the results of physical workouts are easier to see and more immediate – better muscle tone, weight reduction, more energy and, of course, the endorphins coursing through our veins making us feel bright-eyed and bushy-tailed.

Unfortunately, because our brains (hopefully) remain out of sight inside our protective skulls all our life, it is far more difficult to see and experience tangible benefits to better mental health. The brain is hidden from view – you can't see what is wrong or notice improvements as easily.

Nonetheless, it is a medical fact that if we keep our brains healthy then we are far more likely to live longer and happier lives. Of course, with this greater longevity comes a multitude of problems related to ageing – the obvious ones are physical (reduced mobility, disease and illness, and so on), but there is also a massive strain on global health services as a result of the increased mental-health challenges of an older population. Most obviously, this unfortunately means that more of us are falling victim to brain diseases, such as dementia and the horrible Alzheimer's that took my mum's life. It is a trend that looks set to continue for the foreseeable future.

So, having established that brain health is as important as physical wellbeing, how can we improve what is going on in our heads? I'm sure, like me, you have heard neurologists comparing the brain to a muscle, by way of warning us that it will deteriorate if we don't keep working it out. Essentially, we're advised to 'use it or lose it'. This sound advice is usually followed up by little more than suggesting we do crosswords, puzzles and jigsaws – all of which, I hasten to add, are very useful. They certainly do stimulate your brain but we can go much, *much* further than that.

There is actually a lot more that we can do to keep our brains in fine fettle. Indeed, there are many scientists all over the world getting very excited that these relatively new techniques appear to stave off – and in some cases even prevent – dementia, Alzheimer's and other brain diseases.

So, apart from a daily puzzle or word search, how exactly do you exercise your brain? You've almost certainly come across, heard about and maybe even tried aerobics? Well, let me introduce you to Neurobics – *the idea of exercising and improving the fitness of your brain.*

Neurobics is a term originally attributed to the American neurobiologist Lawrence Katz (1956–2005) and Manning Rubin, both early pioneers of brain-training but also co-authors of the brilliant book *Keep Your Brain Alive.* Prior to their work, it was thought that the total number of brain cells we have was 'capped' – in other words, what you were born with was all you were going to get. However, Katz and Rubin's research revealed that the brain is much like other parts of our body in that it can produce *new cells* that can then become a fresh part of the brain's overall function.

Essentially, what Neurobics does is stimulate the brain's ability to produce natural growth – in scientific terms by pro-ducing neurotrophins, otherwise known as brain food! Neurotrophins are proteins found in the bloodstream, and have the capability of allowing brain cells to survive and, perhaps more significantly, to grow. The more active your brain cells, the more neurotrophins are produced. Neurobic exercises are specifically designed and targeted to produce significant quantities of these growth-stimulating molecules.

When it comes to loss of brain function, part of the issue is that modern life has seen us evolve to sometimes use *less* of our brain's capacity rather than more. We have come a long way since our cave-dwelling days, but there are some things we don't do as well now as we did back then.

For example, we don't use all of our senses nearly as much. These days, we rely mainly on just two of them: sound and vision, largely because more of our experiences seem to be visual. Life is so fast-paced now, and our eyes and ears are a lot quicker in telling us what is going on than our other three senses, as well as helping us figure out how best to react and make decisions. Touch, taste and smell (relative to sight and hearing) are utilized far less. In particular, our sense of smell used to be vital for survival. I guess it would have been fairly handy back in the day to have been able to smell a sabre-tooth tiger before it came into vision, or to know that food with a certain aroma might be poisonous. Our ability to smell is potentially under-appreciated – especially as it is said by neuroscientists to still be our biggest 'trigger' to re-connect us to past memories – in particular, those associated with emotion. Whenever I smell a certain perfume – I think it is called Intimate – it triggers memories of an ex-girlfriend from many years ago whose name was Christine. Hello, Christine!

Neurobic exercises encourage you to use ALL FIVE of your senses in new and very different ways, and the benefit of doing this is that it improves your brain's performance. Put in its most simple terms, using all of your senses more often activates rarely used brain pathways and quickly boosts your mental powers – a bit like picking up a TV remote, pointing at a brain and switching the cells that are currently on red (standby) over to green (GO!).

There are obviously several aspects of ageing that we cannot prevent, but the science of neurology suggests that memory loss may not be one of them, and that it is possible to create new neurons that improve thinking as well as memory function. This is where Neurobics comes in. By deliberately engaging your other senses such as touch, smell and taste, Neurobics helps your brain quickly become more active, more powerful and more efficient.

It is never too late to enjoy the benefits of Neurobics, as we now know much more about the brain's plasticity – a common term used by neuroscientists to describe the brain's ability to change at any time. It could be said this neuroplasticity is at the root and heart of all brain-training exercises, thereby keeping our brains healthy so we can continue to learn new skills, activities and languages well into our twilight years, and beyond.

So what exactly are the Neurobic exercises we are talking about? Well, first of all, understand that your brain workouts will all take place in a mental gym – so no membership fees, no big sweaty alpha males straining to intimidate you: this can all be done in your head. You don't have to move from your living room, or even get up. The brain's gym is any place, all around you, right here, right now.

You don't need a personal trainer either, but for the purposes of this book, let me guide you through what Neurobics is and how it can transform your brain's health and power. Let's begin by looking more closely at why we should do more than crosswords, jigsaws and Sudoku puzzles, so that we can all enjoy the extra benefits to be gained from Neurobics.

Give this a go: lay out your clothes neatly the night before, and when you get up in the morning, get dressed with your eyes shut – no peeping. Simply feel each item of clothing and its buttons or zips, your socks and your shoes. By doing this, you will be engaging fully the senses other than sight and will be amazed at how much more engaged in the process you are than usual. You will feel the texture of the clothes, maybe the coldness of the zip, the flex of your shoelaces, the feel and sound of the click of the clasp on your watch strap.

Eyes-closed Neurobics can be practised during other activities that are part of your daily routine, such as showering and eating. In fact, eating a meal blindfolded comes with the extra benefit that you are very likely to eat less as well as boost your brain power – no, not because you might drop most of it down your top, but because you are almost certain to stop eating when you have had your fill.

Staying with touch, have a go at using your non-dominant hand to clean your teeth. Try using this hand to shave your face or legs, although perhaps only if you're using an electric shaver rather than a razor! Or maybe send a text on your phone or use your computer mouse with your non-dominant hand? My favourite 'cross-trainer' Neurobic is to have a go at writing with my non-dominant hand – this is probably the most difficult of all Neurobics, but arguably the most beneficial, because you are writing far more consciously (or, if you prefer, with mindfulness), so you are also boosting your concentration powers – and remember, concentration is the king (or queen) of all mental skills.

Why is changing hands so effective? Because it is well known that the right side of your brain controls the left side of your body, and vice versa. Therefore, when you switch to your non-dominant hand, the other side of your brain is more active and you are switching on rarely used brain cells. It's like turning up the lights in your house using a dimmer switch – the 'new' cells shine more brightly.

Strange as it might sound, turning things such as clocks, pictures, calendars and anything else you can 'flip' upside down is an excellent Neurobic exercise. When you read them this way, your right brain hemisphere dominates rather than your left and this can improve spatial awareness – having an awareness of your relationship with your surroundings. When we are walking, good spatial awareness prevents us from bumping into things. It stops us knocking items off a table, it ensures you keep your car in the correct lane, and it gives you an awareness of traffic around you. It's important and useful whatever your age because we constantly use this cognitive skill.

Reading out loud is a brilliant Neurobic exercise, because when you hear as well as see the written word, you are activating two distinct areas in your right and left brain hemispheres – reading silently only activates one area of the cortex in the left hemisphere.

I would also add any form of meditation to the Neurobic exercise menu, because it is guaranteed to dumb down the left hemisphere where the Monkey lives, giving your brain a well-earned 'pit stop'. In fact, many neuroscientists suggest that meditation is actually better quality rest for your brain than sleep, as well as being good for mental health generally.

And don't forget music – it's better to listen to music with your eyes closed (if it is safe to do so), because you will hear more notes, more nuances, and engage with the melody much more intimately. Crucially, it also utilizes more brain cells, too.

Engaging with, and regularly practising, these Neurobic exercises gives your brain new experiences by using ALL of your senses, not just the dominant ones of sight and hearing. This stimulates more and more connections between different areas of your brain and, just like exercising a muscle in your body, your brain power and strength will grow, and your mental health will remain as fit as a butcher's dog.

Your brain loves new experiences, loves to be challenged – that's how it has evolved and will continue to do so. Keeping your brain on its toes, so to speak, and bringing it out of its comfort zone is the essence of Neurobics.

Neurobic exercising is also beneficial when trying to control our old friend the Monkey Mind. A stronger, fitter brain can deal more easily with excessive anxiety, negative thoughts and feelings, and any Monkey Meltdowns, allowing you to return to your calm sea of mental tranquillity much faster.

So, if you are looking for improved concentration, better moods, reduced anxiety and stress, more creativity and, ultimately, a fun-filled, long life, all this and more is yours – even if you are an old fart like me, Neurobically speaking.

Let Neurobics turbo-charge your brain.

Case Study

Neurobics

Tom

I like working with youngsters because it is possible to teach even very young kids good mental habits, give them some understanding as to why they feel the way they do, introduce them to their own Monkey Minds, and thereby prevent unwanted obstructive thoughts from developing as they get older . . . especially during the teen years!

When Tom's dad brought him to me for some help, I found it very easy to connect with this very likeable young man, and I was soon to be very impressed by the way he applied himself and used the Tools I showed him – in particular Neurobics – to regain control of his emotions and his Monkey Mind, as he explains so eloquently in his story.

I am still in contact with him today and it gives me great pleasure to see that he was/is worth every bit of assistance I was able to give him three years ago. People like Tom are exactly why I do what I do. Great job, Tom!

When I was ten, my dad unexpectedly fell very ill one night. He was in hospital for a week, where he had an operation, and then he returned home to recuperate for three months. Although he was fixed, it had still been a really serious incident that really shocked me. At first I was relaxed about my dad's health, but this changed after a few more months had passed. I started to feel unsettled, with no understanding of why.

At school I started to have panic attacks, triggered by things I saw or heard. For example, one day we were learning about how to react if a family member became suddenly ill with similar problems to what my dad had experienced. This was the first time I really felt the full damage my anxiety could cause: I became very dizzy and panicked, and had to leave the class, even though I was not sure of where to go. I headed to my school's student support section, who were very helpful but I still had to take the rest of the day off. I felt as though when I was triggered I went into a mental lockdown, and it seemed impossible to harness the panic.

Another occasion when this happened was when an air ambulance landed next to the school field. I came down from playing football with my friends to see a huge group of school kids crowded excitedly around the gate to the field. As soon as I saw it,

I asked the school janitor what was the problem and he said, 'A man in town has been taken seriously ill.' My immediate thought was that it must be my dad. I had to sit on the floor and attempt to calm myself down, but by that point I was already panicking. Of course, it wasn't my dad but I found myself off school and at home again.

I began to struggle to focus in class, which in turn affected my learning. I often felt ill with nausea, headaches, shakiness, and so on. These incidents became so frequent that it started to impact on my school attendance, such that in one academic year I was off sick thirty days. I later realized that when I was off school, I would often be calmer because I was with Dad – who works from home – but at the time I genuinely felt ill, it wasn't a pretence.

My parents were understandably worried and decided to speak to Don, having met him through a friend. I hadn't had any previous association with anyone who could help improve my mental wellbeing, so I didn't know what to expect. He offered to FaceTime me, so we spoke about what had happened and what I felt when I had these attacks.

Don was really helpful and explained two major ideas to me: first, he talked to me about the Monkey Mind, and how it had run riot and was causing these panics. My Monkey is called Colin and Don taught me how to be in charge of my thoughts, rather than Colin. Once I started to get the hang of this, I quickly improved my ability to stay calm.

Don also taught me Neurobics and this made a big difference. He got me playing cricket and tennis with my weak hand, as well as getting dressed with my eyes shut and other fun activities! It was really hard at first, but as the right side of my brain began to develop, it got easier and easier. This seemed to really help keep Colin in check.

It has been four years now since my dad was ill, and over a year since my last panic attack. Colin and I are now good partners in balancing my everyday life. I practise what Don taught me, and we still speak occasionally, but just as friends, because he has enabled me to tune my own brain and look after myself independently. Minding the Monkey and Neurobics have changed my life to the point where my anxiety days feel like a distant dream that has no relevance to me any more, other than to boost my confidence in overcoming any future challenges and also to remind me of just how far I have come.

Tool 8

The Immune-system Booster

How to 'Think Yourself Well'

When asked to name a hero, which individual comes to mind first? Winston Churchill? Neil Armstrong? Michelle Obama? We all have our favourites, but there is one name I suggest we should all add to the list – let's hear it for Edward Jenner! Who? I hear you ask.

OK, I'd better come clean and admit I wasn't sure who he was either, although his name was familiar. Edward Jenner (1749–1823) was an English physician who, among other roles, worked for King George IV, but much more than that he is responsible for saving many *millions* of lives, arguably more so than any other person before or since. Why? Because Jenner helped pioneer the vaccine against smallpox, the disease that killed 10–20 per cent of the British population in the eighteenth century.

Jenner's vaccine didn't just reduce the death rate for future generations, ultimately (in 1979) it completely eradicated the disease. Even more crucially, the success of that innovation popularized the use of vaccines globally, and the number of lives saved subsequently is almost impossible to comprehend.

His work also led to many more scientific breakthroughs in the nineteenth and twentieth centuries, and continues to be relevant in today's healthcare systems through the development of vaccines, immunotherapy, the battle against autoimmune diseases, and the fight against emerging new viruses and pathogens such as Ebola, HIV, rabies, influenza and, of course, coronavirus (I am writing this book while in lockdown due to the global Covid-19 pandemic in the spring of 2020).

Known as the 'father of immunology' Jenner was included in a 2002 BBC poll to select the Top 100 Greatest Britons. Tragically, his own wife died from tuberculosis; many years later, his pioneering work ultimately led to the evolution of a TB vaccine that is the most widely used of all immunizations – over 90 per cent of the world's children receive this jab. Enough of a hero for you?

All very interesting, but why do I need to tell you about Jenner in a book about mind management? Simply put, because modern science is now starting to discover that – despite doubts to the contrary for many decades – it might be possible to show that *in certain circumstances and with certain illnesses*, we may be able to 'think' ourselves better.

To explain this in more detail, I need to offer up a science lesson, with today's subject being the immune system. No talking at the back!

Our immune system is a network of cells, organs and tissues all over our body, which work as a team to protect us from infections, diseases, viruses, and so on. It is our physical defence system, often referred to as our 'floating brain' because of its ability to 'talk' to our brain via chemical messages.

Immune-system cells can also be found in the skin, bone marrow, bloodstream and spleen – even in mucosal tissue in the lungs. You could argue that the immune system includes our lungs (containing mucus to cough out germs), acids in our tummies (to kill infections), and let's not forget saliva, tears or bodily fluids such as oil, all of which help reduce our risk of infection.

The immune system's first line of defence is to stop and keep germs, such as bacteria and viruses, from entering our body, but it also has a very effective plan B should any manage to evade detection. Some of the immune-system cells are monitoring our body 'looking for trouble', others simply destroy invaders and threats to our health and wellbeing.

Some particularly clever cells help the body to remember the invaders, in case they have the cheek to come back – rather like your number plate being read by a camera to make sure you don't sneak back early to a free parking space! When your immune system's radar detects an incoming enemy agent returning for another attack, it clocks the 'registration' and gets rid of it for you – this is why some viruses such as chickenpox and mumps (usually) strike only once.

I must confess to being in awe of, and completely fascinated by how powerful, smart and adaptable the immune system is. My own favourite cells are the killer T-cells. They are like the SAS of our own personal armed forces, specially trained to kill the enemy on sight, each one as hard as nails. They really don't mess about. When your immune system is struggling – maybe you're fighting off a cold or you're experiencing a stressful time – the door is left wide open for other harmful infections to sneak in under the radar. But don't fret, other cells spot the invader and contact the SAS killer T-cells, who see the danger and snuff it out rapidly – shock and awe, you might say!

So, your immune system really is the most remarkable physical self-defence mechanism. However, real problems can start when it gets overloaded. This can happen for many reasons, such as fatigue, poor diet and stress. The bad news is that this is when viruses and other nasties can find their way past your 'sentries', and you become poorly, sometimes very poorly. A run-down immune system can lead to increased inflammation inside the body, which leaves us much more prone and vulnerable to all sorts of diseases.

Given that our immune system is so clearly essential to a long and healthy life, what can we do to assist that medical miracle in keeping in good shape? It is common knowledge that exercise, good nutrition and quality sleep (see Tool 9: Better Sleep – page 171) help strengthen our immunity.

There are also many fantastic medical boosts that science can give us in times of need, and preventative assistance such as vaccines. However, is there more we can do? I believe there is.

Bear with me, a little science will explain more . . . We need to talk about our Autonomic Nervous System (ANS), which controls and regulates bodily functions (mostly subconsciously) such as breathing, digestion, blood flow and heart rate. It is also the main mechanism for controlling our 'flight or fight' response.

For many years it has been assumed that it is impossible for us to influence our ANS, but now we have access to more research and experiments that strongly suggest this is not necessarily the case. Indeed, some medical data suggests that we can, and should, influence our ANS.

What relevance does this have to this book, and specifically to this chapter? Well, perhaps most significantly of all, our ANS can talk to our immune system. There is some highly convincing research/evidence that 'focused intense concentration' can, and does, positively affect our immune system. Inflammation markers, which otherwise reduce the power of our immune systems significantly, are reduced, and more of the cells that send messages to my old favourites, the SAS killer T-cells, are produced to destroy infections, diseases, and even ageing to some degree.

I am not going to swamp you with hundreds of references to academic essays and studies. Instead, I want to give you just one of the increasingly encouraging real-world examples that there might be something in the notion of 'thinking yourself' to better health. So hold on – the Iceman cometh.

Wim Hof is a Dutch 'extreme athlete' who holds at least twenty Guinness World Records. He has climbed both Everest and Kilimanjaro wearing only shoes and shorts, and has also run a marathon in 50°C heat, without food or water! He is especially well known for his amazing, record-setting swims under ice-capped water, as well as his astonishing ability to endure prolonged, full-body contact with ice. Hence his nickname – the Iceman.

Perhaps inevitably, Hof has been the subject of several scientific studies, some of which have confirmed his remarkable ability to *consciously control his immune system* by influencing his ANS, mainly through increasing his heart rate and adrenalin levels. According to Hof himself, he focuses on three core elements: lots of exposure training in very cold conditions, special breathing techniques, and focused intense concentration. The overall result is that he significantly reduces harmful inflammation and disease in his body, leading to better health and less illness.

But if the Iceman isn't cool enough for you, let me introduce you to Richard Davidson, Professor of Psychology and Psychiatry at the University of Wisconsin-Madison in the US. As far as I know, he does not hold any Guinness World Records, but he is a good friend of the fourteenth Dalai Lama, a pairing that makes for an interesting mixture of faith and science.

Professor Davidson suggests that there is more to staying

healthy than washing your hands regularly, exercising and eating well. During the course of his research he uses MRI scans to take a detailed look at the brain, and his latest studies seem to confirm a direct link between brain activity and the immune system. In particular, there's evidence that focused concentration produces demonstrably positive effects on both the brain and the immune system by producing higher levels of antibodies, which prevent and fight off illness.

If you're still with me at the back of the class, I'd like to tell you how this might benefit you. Sit tight . . .

The key question here is can we 'think' ourselves well?

Can we control and adjust our immune system?

I believe we can.

My opinion is based not only on reading the science, but also on anecdotal evidence from the many hundreds of clients I have worked with over the course of twenty-five years. Let me give you some brief background on how this technique found its way on to my brain-tuning Tools menu.

Over the years, as I worked with many international sportspeople, I noticed that more and more of them were complaining of succumbing to various ailments while travelling around the world – long-haul flights seemed to be the common denominator in picking up illnesses – and some were catching common colds close to events and competitions. Given this was likely to affect their performance, they wanted to know if there was more they could do to stay fit and well besides taking vitamin supplements, going to the gym, eating sensibly and getting good-quality sleep.

I began to study intently the field of immunology, focusing in particular on how malleable the immune system may or may not be. Through years of study and conversations with medics on the front line of this relatively new theory, I came up with the notion that maybe we could tune our brain to 'talk' to our immune system – to make sure it was working efficiently and to boost the system just when we needed it. In effect, to see if we could deliberately or consciously control and direct the immune system's powers to the areas of our body needing extra care and attention (or even just to keep us healthy more generally).

I began experimenting with several high-profile motor racers, golfers and tennis players, all of whom were flying around the world on a regular basis to compete in prestigious sporting events.

It's how I came up with the idea of an Immune-system Booster.

I asked these sports stars to visualize how their immune system might look inside their body – in any way that pleased them – and then to begin to foster a better relationship with it. In particular I wanted them to learn how to visualize in their mind's eye how their immune system would look if it were working on full power – far too strong to yield to any potential threat to their health, and doing a great job of keeping them fit and well. They were, in effect, waking up their immune system, prompting it to be on heightened alert.

Once they had worked with me on that idea, they would practise my technique in the days leading up to a big competition. We quickly found out that a daily practice was most effective, generally speaking, and, more importantly, always before, during and after a long-haul flight. I also recorded a special 'Talk to Your Immune System' mp3 to help make the practice more accessible, easier to do and effective. I soon began to receive very encouraging feedback, with all manner of clients from different backgrounds telling me that they were convinced this was helping.

The more I studied this emerging field of thought, I realized that my own father had suspected there could be a link between mind management and the immune system. My father, a doctor, was only ever sick at Christmas, and he was convinced it was because his immune system relaxed and opened the door to colds and other illnesses. Have you ever experienced that? How many times have you fallen sick at Christmas, or when you have a holiday, or even a few days off? My dad started to work 'a little' over the Christmas break. I am sure it was to fool his immune system into thinking it was *not* a holiday and therefore to remain vigilant!

The crux of the Immune-system Booster mp3 was something like this, but you can personalize it in any way you feel appropriate:

1. Sit down, or lie down.
2. Get nice and comfortable then keep as still as you can.
3. Switch on your Zen Breathing and ask it to slow down . . . Slow down . . .
4. Close your eyes, if it is safe to do so.
5. Now, imagine your immune system: it is every-where in your body, but where is its headquarters? In your chest area? Your heart? In your tummy . . . ? That is your choice and personal to you. (I see my HQ in the centre of my chest.) Once you decide where it is, visualize it clearly.
6. This is your Churchillian War Room where the commander of your troops (cells) and his highly trained staff are constantly monitoring your health, watching the radar closely for incoming invaders and threats to your health. The regular army of troops is patrolling every part of your body twenty-four-seven, looking for anything suspicious and reporting back to HQ if they do spot something.
7. When the regular army has identified a threat – a sore throat, a cough, inflammation somewhere, a runny nose, perhaps – an urgent message is sent to HQ asking for assistance or back-up. Speed is of the essence to stop the threat from progressing.
8. The commander then sends out the special troops (the SAS) to that part of your body. These are

your immune system's killer T-cells, who are now heading straight for the invader with only one instruction from the commander – 'Destroy!' Can you visualize this scenario inside your body, or something close to it?

9. Other troops (cells) are also deployed to mop up, and you can now see that the target area of previous discomfort is now 100 per cent clear, clean and healthy. How might you visualize this? As a colour, perhaps? Maybe the early throat inflammation was red, and now a pure, perfectly healthy white remains.

10. The final step is to visualize the threat having receded. Your immune system is victorious and all those amazing cells are celebrating their victory!

It can take a good level of focus to imagine this going on in your body, but it's fun to do so, and once you have the idea in your mind, you can switch it on quickly and easily.

This Tool should be practised every day, but especially in advance of occasions when you really need to be feeling tickety-boo and firing on all cylinders – ahead of an important presentation at work or an exam at school maybe, or perhaps you are getting married or have a holiday booked and want to make sure you don't get sick. Indeed, before any big moment in your life when you want to feel 100 per cent.

*

I am a staunch believer in this Tool – you might be encouraged to hear that I have very rarely been ill on important
occasions when I can't afford to be. Am I actually talking to
my immune system during these 'must stay well' times? Am
I really issuing instructions, warning my 'troops' to be on
red alert when I step inside a plane, for example? I believe
so, and my own experience along with the feedback from
many, many clients suggests there is most definitely something of value here.

I recognize that this is an evolving field, and I am also
very clear that I am *not* advocating dismissing conventional
medicine. Some conditions absolutely will not improve with
the use of this Tool – there are some illnesses that will be a
huge challenge even to the greatest medics in the world.
That is an obvious fact and I want to be very clear on the
matter – *you must always work with and alongside medical professionals.*

What I *am* saying is that my Immune-system Booster
Tool is free, easy to learn and accessible to draw on at any
point in your life when you feel you might need a little help
to ensure events go well . . . Why not give it a go? What have
you got to lose?

The Immune-system Booster

Vickie

When I first met Vickie it was clear she was not in a good place. What was also clear was that even though she was struggling through some particularly tough times, her wit, strength and personality still shone through. Her story says it all really, but I would like to add that she has been a wonderful inspiration to many people, including myself. She applied herself to the task of returning to better health with both humour and determination. Several Tools were brought into play during her journey, but I would say the number-one Tool for her was the Immune-system Booster. Her Silver Warrior!

I staggered into the bathroom on weak, shaking legs, clutched the cold rim of the basin and coughed. The resultant splatter of stark, bright red contrasted alarmingly with the brilliant-white porcelain. A blur of paramedics appeared in the room, then nothing.

Over the following hours, as I slipped in and out of consciousness, through the blur, noise and confusion came the realization I was in hospital.

I was in ITU on life support, with multiple-organ failure, waking from a nine-day controlled coma. A ventilator was breathing for me, via a tube inserted down into my chest, which also rendered me speechless. I could turn my head, lift my arms slightly, but otherwise my body – weak, emaciated, yet bloated with fluid – was too heavy for me to move. A nasal feeding tube delivered liquid food down my throat directly into my stomach. My kidneys were reliant on dialysis, and leads inserted into my neck controlled my heart's wayward beating.

A complex autoimmune condition had first manifested itself the previous year and developed aggressively. My hyperactive immune system attacked my body's healthy tissue, causing my muscles to break down and my vital organs to fail. The powerful drugs that were ensuring my survival, along with infection, were wreaking havoc on my mind. In a more lucid moment I mouthed to one of my doctors, 'What are my chances?'

'Fifty-fifty,' he replied. 'I can't say better than that.'

After almost two months in the ITU, still unable to breathe unaided, I was transferred to a specialist lung hospital to be weaned off the ventilator. The anxiety of moving away from the security of the familiar staff and surroundings was exacerbated by another infection and a further week in ITU.

I gradually returned to independent respiration, and by the middle of June was wheeled outside and felt the breeze on my skin for the first time in three months. Now stable, I was transferred back to my local hospital. I wasn't able to sit up, feed or wash myself, but I was gaining strength steadily. I learned to hold a cup, clean my teeth, and took my first wobbly steps in five months.

After six months in hospital, I was wheeled into the familiarity of my home, half my original body weight and a stranger to myself.

From a young age, I was fiercely independent, confident, competitive, spirited and fun-loving. I'd been a sportswoman, and a highly regarded senior manager responsible for million-pound businesses. Now I found myself unable to stand, walk, feed or wash myself. My hair was thin and lifeless. My clothes fell off my emaciated body, yet my face and torso were bloated from the medication I was taking.

My incarceration had also taken its toll mentally, as my mind tried to take in the magnitude of events. I was haunted by vivid flashbacks of my twisted, terrifying dreams, as well as excruciating pain and fear. I was in mourning for my past life, angry at the injustice of it all, and frustrated by the straitjacket of my illness. I was also weighed down with survivor's guilt after hearing that a friend and colleague with a similar autoimmune condition had just died.

Progress was slow and stuttering.

Twelve months later, I was walking a few steps and, despite further bouts of infection requiring additional hospital stop-overs, I expected the worst was over. I was looking forward to getting my life back. I paid little attention to the onset of unfamiliar, fleeting, tingling sensations in my face and arms. I was getting better, after all.

A year to the day since I'd left hospital, the light went out in my right eye. Subsequent tests and neurological assessments revealed my carotid artery was completely blocked and I'd experienced a series of mini-strokes; one in the central retinal artery of my right eye. I was unlikely to regain any vision in it.

After months of steady improvement, hope and looking forward, the news floored me. Hadn't I been through enough already? All-consuming anxiety and fear (the legacy of my ITU terrors) were manifesting as debilitating panic attacks.

Fortunately, Don was recommended to me as 'the best intervener on the autonomic level'. I knew little about him, but with nothing to lose I launched an SOS email into the ether. The following day, my lifeline arrived.

'The cavalry's on its way,' Don replied. Everything was about to change.

After our first conversation, I dared to believe there was hope.

A four-hour car journey and overnight stay in order to meet him was a huge endeavour in itself, taking me hundreds of miles away from the security of the hospital. I was struck immediately by Don's warmth, empathy, gentle positivity and humour. He had a plan, and the first step was for me to 'meet' my immune system.

What did it look like?

I immediately brought to mind a dark, sinister, insidious presence lurking in the shadows, waiting to strike whenever I least expected it.

Then he asked me how I'd like it to be?

A tall, strong, powerful, protective, kind and compassionate figure, dressed in silver armour sprang to mind: my Silver Warrior.

In order to instil my all-new immune system in my subconscious, Don used hypnosis to enable me to reach a state of deep relaxation; a very comforting and liberating experience. From this moment, my Silver Warrior was (and still is) my immune system – my kind, powerful protector.

Don also introduced me to my Monkey Mind, which had become hyperactive, wilful and wayward, bombarding me with negative, fearful thoughts that culminated in panic attacks. But the good news was that my Monkey and my thoughts could be controlled. The route to accessing both my Silver Warrior and Monkey Mind was through correct breathing techniques, which he would teach me.

I left Don, feeling emboldened, with a plan and sense of purpose.

On returning home, despite feeling overwhelmed with fatigue initially, I quickly realized that profound changes were already occurring. I soon felt more energized, both mentally and physically, with a greater sense of being able to cope, and lighter in my mood. All of these sensations had been absent for more than a year.

I caught sight of my reflection in the mirror and recognized myself, as though I fitted in my skin again, which was incredibly uplifting and filled me with confidence. I had taken my first step to learning a new skill and language, and already feeling the benefits I committed to it wholeheartedly.

Inevitably, however, I encountered bumps in the road – when my Monkey Mind couldn't resist returning to its pesky ways and I'd feel overwhelmed again . . . However, with Don's guidance, my physical and mental strength grew as my sense of disconnect faded and I settled into being the new me. I even started driving again. I was having fun and appreciating every moment.

Living with a chronic condition brings daily fluctuations and developments. For me, there was no 'Ta-da, I'm cured!' moment. Instead, my new skills are enabling me to live my life more fully and more contentedly than I dared imagine. I am now in a period of stable health, fitter than before, and happier than I've ever been. My [immune system's] Silver Warrior is constantly at my side, guiding and encouraging me – in Don's voice, of course. It's constantly helping me adapt to and accept my new reality, safe in the knowledge that whatever happens next I have all the Tools I need to cope. I can never thank Don enough, and count myself so incredibly lucky to have met him.

Tool 9

Better Sleep

How to Wake Up Feeling
Refreshed and Reenergized

Sleep is vitally important to us all, for our mental and physical wellbeing. When we can't sleep well, our lives can seem to unravel quickly. The American entertainer, writer and actor W. C. Fields once said, 'The best cure for insomnia is to get a lot of sleep,' and in many ways he hit the nail on the head.

It is an age-old problem that affects millions and millions of people, and has done so for generations. When you aren't sleeping very well, you start to worry about not sleeping very well. You crave a normal night's sleep. This urge then loads bedtime with countless anxieties before you even get to your bedroom. When you put your head on the pillow, you can't stop thinking . . . about the day, about tomorrow, about sleep. You think about everything, even thinking about thinking.

In turn, your lack of sleep means that your moods, day-time decision-making ability and energy levels are impaired. This leads to more stresses and complications, which gives you even more to think about when you finally lie down the following night . . . and so on and so on. If only you could get a few good hours' sleep . . .

We are all aware that we don't always get a decent night's sleep, but perhaps we don't all realize how important it is for our physical and mental wellbeing. One poor night leaves you feeling tired – and most likely irritable – the next day. I don't know about you, but if I have fewer than seven hours' sleep I turn into an even more curmudgeonly, grumpy old git the next day, and my concentration is reduced to that of an ant.

One bad night's sleep is one thing, but weeks and weeks of not sleeping well is a different problem entirely. As the situation gets worse after several rough nights, the effects of poor-quality sleep accumulate and quickly start to impact on your mental capacity in a much more profound way – brain fog, forgetfulness, difficulties in making decisions, a lack of focus and motivation, poor concentration, low moods, fatigue, stress, and even increased clumsiness.

The NHS also tells us that if you suffer from prolonged periods of poor sleep, you can also be at risk of developing more long-term and rather serious health conditions, such as respiratory problems, heart disease and diabetes. NHS advice also states that 'people who sleep less than seven hours a day tend to gain more weight and have a higher risk of becoming obese than those who get seven hours of slumber. This is believed to be because sleep-deprived people have reduced levels of leptin (the chemical that makes you feel full) and increased levels of ghrelin (the hunger-stimulating hormone).'

The data also suggests a heightened risk of anxiety and depression. Even your life expectancy can be shortened. Aside from the longer-term issues mentioned above, there is further evidence that poor sleep compromises your immune system. It's feasible that if you always seem to get every cough and cold going, then poor sleep could be at least partly to blame.

The problem is compounded by the fact that we sleep for about one-third of our lives, a fact that still amazes me. It means I have been out for the count for twenty-three years of my life. As far as I am aware, only Winston Churchill, Margaret Thatcher, horses and elephants can survive on four hours' sleep a night. All well and good for the horses and elephants without much to do the next day, but Winnie and Maggie had to win wars and elections, and make vitally important decisions every single day.

I'm damned if I know how they managed it. I can't help but wonder if things might have turned out any better or differently if they had doubled their sleep quota?

All jokes aside, the 'one-third' statistic means that if you sleep poorly, that is a HUGE chunk of your life that isn't working in your favour.

Let me start this Better Sleep Tool by reassuring you that

if your sleep habits are not ideal, then you are not alone: surveys and research from all over the world continue to confirm that more and more of us simply aren't getting enough shut-eye.

I could pick one of thousands of appropriate studies, some more academic than others, but as an example, a survey by the Mental Health Foundation (which was the largest ever study of the UK's sleeping habits) offered some startling results: 36 per cent of the UK population suffers from possible 'chronic insomnia' to the point that it is affecting their health; of those in the insomnia category, nearly 80 per cent reported having had these problems for over two years; and only 38 per cent of those surveyed were classified as 'good sleepers'.

Although the medical profession is very good at acknowledging the problems caused by a lack of sleep, the support networks are not always there – one client of mine who was an insomniac went to see her doctor, who simply told her to 'stop worrying about not sleeping – it won't kill you'! Advice I would call unsympathetic at best and, at worst, downright damaging.

This dismissive attitude is reflected in wider society, in that anyone who admits that they struggle to get good sleep will inevitably and endlessly be offered advice stemming from thousands of old wives' tales. Some of which are rooted in good science, others which are frankly ludicrous, but all of which can often do nothing but add to the sense of anxiety and pressure around bedtime.

My own clinical experience endorses this notion that poor sleep is a widespread problem. Over the last twenty-five years or so, more and more of my clients have sought help for various sleep-quality issues. Formula One racers who couldn't sleep the night before a race, surgeons who lie awake all night before operating in theatre, and other bad sleepers such as TV presenters facing auditions for big new programmes, students taking exams, and so on . . . None of whom can possibly be at their very best if they are unable to sleep properly.

So there are many good reasons as to why you need to get a good night's sleep and plenty of evidence to suggest that this is a significant problem for much of society. Similarly, it is crystal clear that the benefits of a great night's sleep are enormous – the question is, how do you go about getting those magic seven hours of peaceful slumber?

There are two stages to my advice in this chapter: the first is a well-documented set of rules, commonly referred to as sleep hygiene, that are worth repeating here. The second is my own approach to getting a fantastic, refreshing and rejuvenating night's sleep, by learning about and utilizing your sleep psychology.

Sleep hygiene is essentially loading the odds in your favour of getting good sleep. We all know the obvious ones, such as avoiding drinking caffeine later in the day (the exact cut-off point appears to be a personal thing, but no later than mid-afternoon seems wise). Alcohol might make you feel drowsy, but it will then disrupt your sleep in the middle of the night as the body fights off the effects and you will find yourself awake in the early hours. Not watching stimulating or scary films or TV late at night is certainly sensible, as is avoiding devices and screens for a certain time before bed.

Eating too late also seems to be a commonly quoted factor in disturbing sleep efficiency as your digestive system will still be too active when you are trying to fall asleep. Making sure your bedroom is free of all light and noise is also a good idea and a simple measure you can put in place to stack the odds in your favour.

So take a moment to analyse your habits and routines and make these changes now, otherwise you are already sabotaging your chances of getting that fabulous kip that you so deserve.

Assuming that you have paid good attention to your sleep hygiene and night-time routine, I believe there is even more we can do to improve the quality of our sleep. We can understand and use sleep psychology, which will nicely complement sleep hygiene, allowing us to wake up feeling full of beans, fully reenergized and ready to enjoy the day to come.

Sleep psychology frames the way we think about *why* we sleep, or *why we can't sleep*, which can have a massive influence on allowing you, or preventing you, from entering the wonderful, mysterious Land of Nod. An understanding of your own personal sleep psychology will help you work out why you might not be sleeping very well (if at all), and with this improved awareness you can tailor your strategy to a bespoke solution that could change your life.

To deepen your understanding of your own sleep psychology, we need to analyse what is actually happening when you fall asleep each night. Many years ago, people believed you fell into a state of 'shutdown', then woke up hours later. However, modern science has taught us that sleep is much more complicated and layered than that.

Science has discovered 'sleep cycles', of which there are four. Stage 1 is the light sleep stage. You can be woken easily at this point, but within minutes of dropping off your eye movements slow down; Stage 2 is still quite light, but your brainwaves begin to slow down; Stage 3 is when deeper sleep commences, with slower brainwaves, no eye movement or muscle activity. It is harder for you to be woken and your body is less responsive to the outside world. The final fourth stage is so-called rapid eye movement sleep (REM), which you appear to enter around ninety minutes after nodding off. Each REM phase lasts around an hour, with the average adult experiencing around five or six REM cycles each night.

The question is, can we use this knowledge to improve our own sleep patterns? Put simply, yes! Let me give you an example. My grandmother, Rose Bond, seemed to have magical mental powers when it came to sleep. For starters, she always slept 'like a log', and was happy and energized every morning. Also, she never ever used an alarm clock. If she needed to be up and fully awake at 7 a.m., then all she did was programme her brain to instruct her body to wake up. When she got into bed, she said she quite literally visualized on her forehead the time she wanted to 'rise and shine', then closed her eyes and, to my knowledge, it never failed her. Many years later, and after countless sessions about poor sleep with people from all walks of life, I have come to the conclusion that there is a lot of benefit to be derived from the kind of brain-programming that my grandmother Rose employed.

So, let me drill down into the core of my advice about sleep – and guess who I am going to blame? Yes, you guessed it, your Monkey. Too much Monkey Business when you are hoping to sleep is the key. Over and over again I hear clients saying, 'I just couldn't stop thinking about all sorts of stuff', 'I worry so much about things instead of sleeping', and so on. This is all highly inappropriate and very untimely Monkey Chatter. Of course, there are other things besides unwanted Monkey Chatter that can significantly affect sleep quality, such as illness, pain, and sleep conditions such as apnoea (when breathing is briefly and repeatedly interrupted during slumber).

Also, people who suffer with chronic insomnia would be wise to talk to their doctor. I believe in working closely with the medical profession and therefore strongly recommend that if you really feel you need a helping hand, share your concerns with your doctor, who can discuss the numerous ways they may be able to intervene – with medication, if appropriate.

That said, assuming you have been diligent regarding

sleep hygiene and don't have underlying health issues, I am going to lay the rest of the blame for poor-quality sleep on that pesky primate, the Monkey Mind.

The Monkey can sabotage your sleep so easily at night because you are a sitting duck – in bed, not moving (much), no distractions except maybe the loud snoring of your partner next to you. You can reach for earplugs to block out the snoring, but you can still hear the Monkey rattling on . . . and on and on and on . . .

I know from difficult personal experience how debilitating poor sleep can be, because my monkey Mike's interference with my sleep goes way back. Around 2008 I was working at a hell of a pace, finding it difficult to say no to people and not Feathering the Brakes as I should have been (see Tool 6: Feathering the Brakes – page 121). On top of this frantic work pace, a serious family health worry reared its ugly head, one that appeared to have no solution. So, to be fair to Mike, he had plenty on his mind, so much that it overflowed into the night to the point where, for a period of many long, exhausting months, I completely lost my sleep. (You'll find more details of my experience at the end of this chapter, as a case study.)

Having recovered from this very testing period, Mike is actually very accommodating when it comes to letting me go to sleep these days, but a total pain when I need to get back to sleep on returning from a night-time visit to the bathroom. A typical chat with Mike in the middle of the night would go something like this:

Mike: 'Hey, you, I want to talk to you about the session tomorrow . . . And did you send that email to your accountant, like you promised?'

Me: 'Not now, Mike . . .'

Mike: 'Yes, now . . . And while I have your attention, did you pay the VAT? What have you got for Jane's birthday?'

Me: 'Shut up, Mike!'

Me (to myself): 'If I don't do something to quieten down Mike, the next time I look at the clock it will be too close to getting-up time . . .'

And then it's happened all over again.

Using feedback from clients over years of sessions, and having full empathy with them because of my own challenging times, I have deduced that when it comes to the ways the Monkey can ruin your sleep there are three main areas that we need to look at:

1. The time taken for the Monkey to shut up and 'let you' *go* to sleep.
2. If you wake during the night, the time taken for the Monkey Chatter to cease so you can *get back* to sleep.
3. If you wake *too early*, for whatever reason, and you can hear the Monkey saying, 'It's not worth going back to sleep now, it's too close to getting up, no chance, forget it,' even though you know you've not had nearly enough sleep.

The great news is that the techniques needed to remedy these three sleep problems are interchangeable. ALL three issues can be resolved with one or more of the techniques that I am about to share with you.

Let's begin by being a little fairer to the Monkey, because it is only doing its job by keeping you safe during the day. When life starts to speed up, it (as we have discussed) can become a bit overloaded, and start to encroach on your sleep time by trying to use this time to find answers to questions and solutions to problems. Unfortunately, this just makes matters worse, so you need to manage your Monkey Mind in order to get better sleep.

The only time you don't hear the Monkey in your head is when your conscious mind finally crashes out and you are actually asleep. This is when your subconscious mind, the Night Porter, takes over and makes sure you stay alive by keeping your lungs working, your heart beating, and adjusting other bodily functions such as digestion. Then, around seven hours later (hopefully), the Night Porter's shift finishes and the Monkey Chatter starts all over again as you wake up.

Let's look closer at how we can persuade the Monkey to stop chattering when we wish to sleep, and let the Night Porter take over more easily. The solution is to find better ways of managing the Monkey not just during the day, but also at night. Don't forget, the brain is programmed to take the sleep it needs, if you let it – Mother Nature wants the same result that you do. Now you have a better knowledge of the psychology of sleep . . . what's the plan?

To get to sleep without the Monkey chattering on and on and on, you can apply all the elements of sleep hygiene to tell your Monkey that you are in control and heading towards a great night's sleep no matter how much it wants to rattle its cage.

I would advise using the Zen Breathing Tool – or, indeed, practising any form of meditation – reading, listening to soothing music, watching nature programmes on TV . . . Whatever you choose, the effect must be to calm the conscious Monkey Mind down as much as you can. By taking steps to assert control of your Monkey before bedtime, it will be more relaxed and amenable to letting the Night Porter take over when you hit the sack. If you take a restless, unmanageable Monkey to bed with you, it's going to be much tougher to crash out – sleep is a dance, not a wrestling match.

Take your time when getting undressed, cleaning your teeth, putting your night clothes on, and so on. It will help you maintain a feeling that you, not the Monkey, are in control of sleep. Your body language needs to be deliberately calm, relaxed and confident, sending a strong message to the Monkey that all is well. Set up any sleeping aids you choose to use, such as earplugs, maybe something comfortable to cover your eyes, and anything else that allows you to attract sleep, and block out external distractions.

Now you are in bed and it is time to sleep. You've done a cracking job with all the relevant sleep hygiene tips, which in itself boosts your confidence that you can nod off. Now it's time to add the sleep psychology.

If you are going to bed with a cluttered mind, the trick is to declutter it. In order to do that, we need to KEEP IT SIMPLE. I am going to suggest you use only three techniques: Stop Trying, Zen Breathing and Hollywood Movie.

The first thing to do is STOP TRYING. This may sound like an odd statement but it is a fact that actively trying to sleep will certainly fail. The trick is to LET yourself sleep. You simply have to get out of your own way and let sleep come, because it sure as hell wants to! You cannot force yourself to sleep just as you cannot force yourself to relax.

Put ALL of your focus gently but firmly on the process of going to sleep: let the Zen Breathing help you to relax and, after a while, when you can feel that sleep is coming, switch your focus to your body. Visualize every part of your body and use each out-breath to relax every muscle, one by one. You can do this randomly or you can choose to do one muscle group at a time. Whatever approach you use, stay anchored to your breath and to your body.

If the Monkey attempts to interrupt, simply return your attention to your body, time after time after time . . . It's magic and works beautifully, if you LET it. To go to sleep you need to stop the Monkey from dragging you back into the past or pushing you into the future. You need to think of the 'now', which is the process of your conscious mind falling asleep. It is essential that you bring the Monkey into the now by Zen Breathing and using the 'biofeedback' of relaxing each muscle group as described above. Don't worry if you do start to drift off and the Monkey chips in, just persevere: it is a process, and if you follow these instructions you *will* succeed. Sleep *will kick in*, because the brain is programmed that way.

Often, the moment you think it's not working is likely to be the exact moment you drift off . . . Stay with the process, not the result. It might help to add mantras to the out-breaths of your Zen Breathing, such as 'I am calm and relaxed' or – one of my favourites – 'Relax and let go'.

Letting sleep come to you is like trying to catch a butter-fly on a warm summer's day – the more you chase it, the further it moves away from you, but if you sit down, keep still, and slow your breath right down, there is a good chance the butterfly will come to you and settle gently on your shoulder.

If you find that you are still being challenged when it is time to sleep, you have the option of ramping up your approach by utilizing the Hollywood Movie Tool (see Tool 4 – page 87). In this context, you can write, produce and direct a film about yourself going to bed in the most beautiful, relaxed way, or snuggling up in a warm log cabin and dozing off in front of a crackling fire. Alternatively, you can adopt a different angle by creating a movie that is a fantastic distraction, such as having dinner with a famous celebrity, winning an award on the TV – frankly, anything that allows you to vividly create a mind movie. Both approaches will distract the Monkey and lull it into letting you remain in control of your mind and sleep.

One final word – the advice above will be habit-forming. In the same way that you are in the habit of letting the Monkey interfere and grill you with a million questions as you try to sleep, in time you will come to sense when the Monkey is about to shout. You will know how to stop it, and will be able to return yourself to a calm and relaxed state of mind, totally ready for sleep.

So keep practising. The results will accumulate, and before long you will be heading towards each night's sleep with relish, knowing that you are about to enjoy seven or eight hours of absolutely amazing, replenishing sleep. You are in control, not the Monkey, and good sleep hygiene combined with your knowledge of sleep psychology and these techniques will give you a quality sleep that you could only previously have imagined.

Sleep is beautifully simple if you let it be . . .

Better Sleep

Don

As I mentioned earlier, the case study for the Better Sleep Tool is very personal to me – in fact, it is me! A number of years ago, I was working crazy hours most days to build up my mind-coaching clientele. I had managed to morph from manager to mentor, and was finally engaged in my true passion – helping people to be the best they can be, whoever they are, whatever they do.

Initially my work was centred around elite sportsmen and -women, but the client base branched out inevitably to include, well . . . everyone, really! As the business blossomed, the problem was that I wasn't very good at saying no, and wanted to please everyone. I became so wrapped up in my work that I didn't notice my Monkey, Mike, was taking over my life. Eventually he took over my sleep too.

In addition, a member of my family had a rather worrying health concern, which gave Mike something else to fret about. Consequently, I completely lost my sleep quality, which led to me being more and more tired every day. I simply had to get some energy back, and was only too aware of how poor-quality sleep could threaten my health. Things got so bad that my appetite all but disappeared, even though I continued to work (this is when I should have used my Feathering the Brakes Tool).

I decided I needed some help physically, so I worked closely with my local GP and began to take appropriate medication to give me enough energy to start to regain control of my sleep and my appetite. The first thing I did was STOP TRYING to sleep, get out of the way and let the process unfold – easier said than done, of course! I then introduced the Zen Breathing, which worked its magic, and backed it up with a Hollywood Movie of somewhere relaxing – usually a beach.

Mike still attempts to sabotage my sleep occasionally (particularly if I wake up in the night), because it is all Monkey Business one way or another, but I am ready for him when he does.

Tool 10

The Anxiety Buster

Your Personal Mp3

I suspect some of you reading this book are so anxious that you might think that the Tools described so far are not going to work for you. Maybe you fear they are not immediate enough, or effective and impactful enough. Perhaps you are looking for a quick fix – a silver bullet. Well, let me reassure you that I, and many thousands of others, know exactly how you are feeling. Truly, you are not alone.

Now, I do not claim – or wish – to eliminate anxiety from your life altogether. It is true that a little bit of stress can be helpful in making sure we are ready to perform at our best for a test or exam, or to warn us that something needs checking or doesn't feel right . . . Anxiety is never far away and often for a good reason. I'd love to tell you it diminishes with old age, but it doesn't, it just changes shape as you start to worry about different things. Let me say this right now: you can – and will – control your anxiety, rather than have it control you.

Modern society brings with it so many sources of stress: the pace of life, the internet and social media, peer pressure, health worries and financial troubles, to name but a few. However, in my experience, the worst type is when you have an unresolved worry or issue to which there appears to be no immediate answer.

When a cause of anxiety – a stressor – has been clearly identified and has a beginning, a middle and an end to it, it is much easier to deal with, compared with something that persists and remains unresolved. For example, if you are anxious about a visit to the dentist tomorrow morning, you know that by tomorrow evening, all will be well again. On the other hand, a worry that has been dragging on for a while already, for which no resolution seems to be on the horizon (such as a chronic health concern or a persistent lack of financial security), is something else altogether.

Even the root of the word 'anxious' comes from the Latin 'anxius', meaning to be worried about something uncertain happening in the future. In other words, it's the 'what ifs' that plague so many of us. Unfortunately, our Monkey Mind doesn't like dealing with any level of un-certainty. It demands answers *right now* and doesn't want to know *what* you are going to do about it, but also *when* and *how*.

Your Monkey can become increasingly agitated if no

answer to the 'what if' is forthcoming, and the longer this impasse continues, the closer the Monkey gets to throwing a wobbler, sending your body a rush of unnecessary adrenalin until your appetite disappears, your sleep is destroyed and you feel trapped by constant Monkey Chatter. 'Analysis paralysis' has taken hold and, for now, decision-making is put on hold and your head is full to the brim of thoughts and questions. The Monkey is in charge of your life. Your brain is now burning itself out as the Monkey works overtime, desperately trying to find answers to the issues you are experiencing.

The problem here is that people can feel lost and bewildered because they simply do not understand what is happening or why they feel so dreadful, and they begin to worry that they might never feel like themselves again. In so doing, they are inadvertently creating a negative circle of fear, essentially worrying about worrying.

Once the Monkey has taken charge in this way, you won't be able to perform at your best – it will be hard to focus, you will probably not be sleeping well or eating sensibly, and you'll find it hard to keep a sense of perspective. In short, anxiety can affect every single area of our lives and be all-consuming.

This we must stop, and we shall.

I am confident that I can accelerate your recovery and help reduce your anxiety to much more manageable levels so that you can enjoy your life and be the very best version of yourself every day.

How?

I have a gift for you.

My Anxiety Buster mp3.

Some twenty years ago I came to the realization that the one-to-one sessions I was holding with my clients might have their limitations. I gave these individuals the nine Tools that I have given you so far, and their feedback was that these techniques were transformative and yielded the most remarkable results. Sure enough, people did seem to leave my office feeling reassured that they now had some Tools to help them tune their brains and deal more effect-ively with whatever issue they needed assistance with – but I began to wonder, how long would it be before the benefits of the one-to-one session wore off?

I used to watch clients walk down my drive after a mind-coaching session, invariably switch on their phones again (often before they'd even got into their car), and wander back to their lives. I realized that it would not be long before they would need to attend to a problem, or do something 'urgent', or be involved in a challenging situation . . . and at that point, they would be essentially on their own. It was impossible for me to be present twenty-four hours a day, seven days a week for any of my clients. I was concerned that the great progress we were making in our sessions might be lost amidst the hustle, bustle and generally frantic demands of modern life.

So I got to thinking: what else could I provide for them

that would reflect the essence of the sessions, maintain the momentum, but most importantly of all, remind them of the Tools we had identified to deal with their particular challenges?

That's when I realized that they needed their own personal Anxiety Buster mp3: an audio file recorded by me, talking them through the most relevant parts of my approach to mind management. They could listen to it as often as they liked, anywhere, at any time.

For the next few months, after each client had left my office, I would sit down, quietly reflect on the content of the session and begin to jot down notes that would make up the content of the mp3. Then I would take my dogs for a walk to relax and to see if anything else that would improve my reflections popped up from my subconscious into my conscious mind. On my return I would decamp to my studio where I have a mixer, pick up the microphone . . . and I was off!

I was in the privileged position of working with Formula One racing drivers who agreed to 'test drive' my early attempts at these Anxiety Buster mp3s. One of the racers was, unsurprisingly, struggling to get some quality sleep the night before a grand prix; another wanted to improve his concentration. Both wanted to improve lap times by visualizing an entire lap of the race track at which they were due to be racing soon.

So this mp3 I want to share with you has been honed and refined by feedback from some of the world's greatest sporting heroes. Many of my clients told me they found the mp3 recordings life-changing, and naturally I was delighted with their feedback! At first, the technology I was working with was pretty primitive. I had to record the whole file in one go, which created some very frustrating hiccups when I made a mistake just before the end! On top of that, each CD (remember those?) had to be put inside a jiffy bag, taken to the local post office and sent by recorded delivery at the cost of £5 each time! Luckily, technology makes my life a lot easier now. I estimate that I have recorded in excess of four thousand mp3s over the years, so I think I'm getting the hang of them now.

And so, this is my gift to you – if you follow the link provided on page 237 you will find a free download of my Anxiety Buster mp3 that will talk you through the best and most powerful elements of this book.

Your mp3 Anxiety Buster is a twenty-minute audio file that contains a guided relaxation and visualization, and covers many of the elements of the Tools we have talked about. Anyone of any age, in any country, with access to the internet or in possession of a smartphone can utilize this audio.

I call the mp3 the Anxiety Buster because it allows you to have these Tools to hand at any time to combat the all-encompassing challenge of anxiety. Finding solutions for my clients is very rarely, if ever, done with just one Tool. In almost all cases, three or four Tools work in harmony, and on many occasions an even greater combination is required.

The Tools

This modular structure has been likened to a 'pick-and-mix' approach, where you can choose the Tools that suit you best. With your own personal mp3, you can listen in and remind yourself of the elements that make up your own selection, and each time you do that you are reinforcing a bespoke plan of action in your mind.

So, use the link on page 239, find a nice quiet spot and listen to your own personal audio file. Remind yourself of everything we have talked about, and relax in the knowledge that with all these Tools at your disposal, *you yourself are about to become the most brilliant Anxiety Buster.*

Case Study 1

The Anxiety Buster

Olly

By way of illustrating how important it is to use this 'pick-and-mix' approach, I'd like to highlight three clients of mine who were able to use their mp3 and a variety of Tools to overcome some quite significant issues.

First up, Olly, who was fifteen when he came to see me. I instantly liked him, despite the fact that he thought I was crazy and prehistoric (probably right with both descriptions, to be fair!). I could see a lot of a much younger me in him, as neither of us had much interest in school and ever wanted to be there. Besides our slight age gap, there was one major difference between Olly and me – he is dyslexic, whereas I was disinterested and lazy. (I have worked with several dyslexic youngsters and even visited specialist schools that cater to boys with learning issues.)

As Olly will tell you, understandably he was somewhat cynical about seeing this crazy old mind coach, but was prepared to give it a go – whatever 'it' was! Olly is another member of the Anxiety Busters. Along with his mum we used most of the Tools, and together created a master plan to help Olly through his school years.

Our plan culminated in a personal mp3 recording that allowed him to take control and responsibility for his challenges at school progressively – 'Captain Olly'. Olly says he 'owes me', which is kind of him to say so, but I think I owe him because I reckon he taught me as much, if not more.

His real mind coach, his mum, will tell you how Olly gradually improved and found new and creative ways of learning and winning at school – and life.

Our son Olly is the second of our four boys. It has always been a bit challenging for Olly because he was diagnosed with dyslexia when he was about eight, and school was never his cup of tea. Dyslexia makes learning that much harder, and he has always had to work twice as hard as his older brother, who sailed through school and got top grades.

Olly has never really liked going to school, preferring the outdoors – working on the farm, shooting – and being at home. As he progressed through the education system, he tried with his schoolwork but more out of obligation towards us, his parents, who were paying the school fees, than because he enjoyed it or wanted to be there. As time went by and he started the first of his two years of GCSEs, we felt he was becoming more and more disillusioned. His work seemed to be getting worse and worse, but – most worryingly – he seemed very down and depressed by it all. With only a year to go before sitting his exams, my husband and I decided that we needed to understand what was going on because as things were looking, it seemed like he was going to flunk them.

I scheduled a meeting with his tutor and head of house. Olly attended as well, and the four of us sat down in a meeting room to talk about all his subjects. The tutor was in the process of giving him feedback while the head of house (a lovely man) was trying to push Olly to see what he wanted to do post-GCSEs. Unfortunately, the pressure of the meeting got to Olly and he ran out of the room in floods of tears. We all sat there for a while, expecting him to come back, but he never did. We searched the campus and eventually found him. Seeing how upset he still was, I took him home and left the subject well alone.

It was at this point that we understood that we had a real problem on our hands. Despite having spent a fortune on school fees up to that point, we realized that was no guarantee of anything. It wasn't the school's fault, but a combination of things: we hadn't picked up on how much Olly had slipped and how unhappy he was, so we had to do something about it before it was too late.

My husband had heard of Don through one of his colleagues. This man was absolutely raving about what several sessions with Don had done for his son. I don't really remember the details – I think the boy was a particularly talented rugby player who went through a tough time and Don got him back on his feet. He went on to do really well. We decided that it was worth a shot and I reached out to Don.

I never found out what Olly and Don said to each other during their session (which is totally fine, as it has to be confidential and the child/client has to feel safe to open up without it being passed back to the parents). All I can say is that they hit it off really well and Olly seemed very pleased with the meeting. Don was going to prepare an mp3 recording for Olly to listen to daily, which would prompt him to use the Tools to refocus himself.

Don started off with recordings to build Olly back up as a person. Then, as time went by, the recordings became more geared towards revision and learning the syllabus, without being specific. It was more about encouraging and teaching Olly how to learn and retain the information. Don reconnected Olly with himself. Olly listened to the recordings regularly and I spent time with him building up his revision so that we could break the mountain of material he had to learn into manageable chunks. Don gave us lots of tips on how to do that, and advised us on books about techniques to improve memory and retain information.

We used many of the tips and ploughed through Olly's work. At first, I had to sit down with Olly and do it with him, but as time progressed he took ownership of it and did it all on his own. He had regained his confidence, his motivation, and he started believing that he could actually do it. He revised for his exams all by himself and sat them all. We were absolutely delighted with his results: he got a couple of A*s, lots of As, a B and a C. They were fantastic results, and he totally deserved them.

We would never have expected these results a year prior to that, when I sat in that horrible meeting and my child ran out of the room. The turnaround was beyond phenomenal and we owe such an enormous debt of gratitude to Don. He definitely turned Olly into a Warrior and gave him the Tools for life. We will be forever grateful for his input into Olly's journey.

Olly's Own Account

To put it bluntly, school was s**t. I sort of understood what was going on in lessons, but I could never get it right when I had to do the homework after class. Because I wasn't getting the results I felt I should be getting, I was turning my head further away from school and more towards what the rest of the world could offer. The only trouble was that I was fifteen, and you can't get far or do much at that age.

Every day I went into school feeling incredibly demotivated. I focused on just about everything bar what any teacher had to offer. I stopped enjoying even the sport at school, which was very unlike me. I was going home hating every part of the completely flawed school system. That's when my parents started to look seriously for someone who could help.

I remember the name Don being mentioned as a mind coach, something that I had never heard about. Of course, being in the generation that I am, I looked him up and with a website that didn't look like much at all, I went into his home expecting to return to school as if nothing had occurred. However, something special had occurred in the small room that we sat in for the next two hours.

Don wasn't a teacher, and he wasn't an old-fashioned 'work harder, you're just lazy' kinda man – he was on my level. Bit by bit he won my trust. Eventually, he suggested a method of meditation that might help me. Together, we spent a while going through things such as what made me happy and what drove me. We planned this mp3 recording that I could listen to twice a day to try to motivate me. I left the session feeling as if I'd met a big kid who was there to help.

The next day at school was better – I knew there was someone out there who did understand me – but it didn't change how things were. That evening, an email came through from Don, with the recording. I listened to it and I guess this is the moment when you all expect me to say that things changed . . .

Mmmm . . . kind of. The mp3 definitely helped, but it wasn't 'listen to it once and your life will change'. It was twice a day for twenty minutes each time, and things did change slowly. After a while I went back for another session, just to talk to the crazy mind-coach guy with the prehistoric website again, and to get another more relevant mp3 made. This one was related more to my upcoming exams, but also more general in many ways. It gave me a Tool that could help me in more than just school.

Don was not the sole reason for my turnaround, and he is humble enough to say that I made the changes, not him, but he definitely contributed to my turning the corner at that stage of my life. So, to you, Don, I owe a big thank-you.

Case Study 2

The Anxiety Buster

Patricia – How I Became a Monkey Tamer

Patricia came to me through a mutual friend, and initially asked for some assistance to quit the ciggies. This was a job for my clinical hypnosis training, and I am pleased to report it was an immediate success. What Patricia didn't tell me was that her life then was full of particularly challenging situations, to put it mildly. To be quite honest, I was amazed she had coped thus far without much support. When she came back to see me a few years later (still a non-smoker), it all came tumbling out. She told me she had reached a point where she felt that 'her world was falling apart' – it wasn't, but I'm not at all surprised it seemed that way to her.

On top of all the highly stressful situations she was dealing with, Patricia also told me she worked in a stressful job caring for vulnerable people. This meant that not only had her poor old Monkey Mind been on 'red alert' for a good many years already, but it also had an extra stressful daily workload. Patricia must have felt like a battery gradually losing power, while simultaneously hearing her increasingly worried Monkey screaming at her to 'do something about it'.

Inevitably, the time soon came when she felt 'physically and mentally exhausted'. Patricia has her own delightful way of describing how she dealt with her exhaustion, but in reality she used practically every Tool in the Tool Box, including personal mp3s . . . She became her own brain-tuner and is now a fully fledged Anxiety Buster.

It's December and I am broken. To say that the last few years have had their ups and downs would be an understatement. Some years previously, my partner set fire to our home and then attempted to take his own life . . . That was Monday. On Friday, I collected him from the mental-health unit where he had been for *five* days and was told to 'keep an eye on him'. I went home and that night, as I lay in bed, I wondered if my daughter and I were safe. My world was falling apart and I felt numb.

The next morning I awoke and my partner seemed OK, but my daughter was not. She had lost everything she owned except the clothes that she had been wearing on the day of the fire. She declared tearfully that life was rubbish, she had no toys, we had no festive decorations, and Christmas was going to be rubbish, too.

I was desperately trying to play happy families and pretend that everything was going to be OK. I suggested we all go to a local shopping mall to do some Christmas shopping. She seemed placated as I promised her that nothing else bad would happen. I dried her eyes and we headed out for some retail therapy.

I don't know how many times I have replayed those words in my head over the last few years. Four hours later I received a phone call from my brother to say that my father was in an air ambulance on the way to hospital. By the end of that week, I'd lost my home, everything I owned, my partner (as I knew him) and my father.

This was not what broke me, although at times I thought it would. I survived the trauma of losing my father, the anger I felt that he had left me when I needed him most, and the nagging thought in the back of my mind that the stress of what my partner had done had caused the fatal heart attack. I also coped with the subsequent discovery that my partner, who had been responsible for us losing so much, had been having an affair. I survived all of this . . . but what actually broke me in the end was worry.

I had always been a worrier. I would stay awake all night fretting over whether I'd returned all my library books. I would worry about what might happen if a chain of other events happened, how it might make something awful happen, or as I prefer to call it now 'disastrophizing'. It's not actually a word but it should be.

That December, when I finally broke, I was not sleeping or eating. I was crying, I didn't want to go out, I didn't want to see anybody. I was driving too fast just to see what would happen. I was almost taunting Fate. I was working with vulnerable adults. I loved my work, but the helplessness of some of the things I had to deal with and the situations that some of these people were in were horrendous.

The day I really broke was the day after first-aid training. I had been learning CPR. I kept thinking about my father and how my brother couldn't save him. Somehow, this was enough to bring everything crashing down. Looking back, I'd been on the edge for months, almost manically busy because while I was occupied my mind couldn't keep thinking all the bad stuff that was in my head. I was running from the 'black dog' of depression and anxiety. If I kept busy enough, if I drank a bit more, I could keep going, but mentally and physically I was exhausted.

I went into work that day and started crying, and I couldn't stop. I couldn't see a way out of how I felt. As far as I was concerned, nobody could help me. Signed off work and staying with my mother, I was in a bad way.

In desperation and despair, my mother suggested I go back and see the Monkey Whisperer. He'd helped a good friend of ours, and some years earlier had helped me stop smoking. From that day I always sang Don's praises whenever the opportunity arose. Such was my glowing praise that my mother saw him as a miracle worker. Now that I was struggling so much, she thought that he might be able to hypnotize me better.

I rang Don and he agreed to see me a few days later. As the day of our session approached, I realized that I really did not want to go and see him. I didn't want to talk to anybody else about the stuff going on in my head. I had talked to my mum and my friends, and I was fed up with talking about it all – it was making things worse. I couldn't bear the thought of talking to one more person about it. Nobody could fix me, nobody could help me.

I went to the session because Don had been good enough to fit me in, and I guess my good manners wouldn't let me cancel when he had gone out of his way to make time to see me.

Had I not have gone, I really don't know if I would be writing this today.

So . . . what magic did he do, how can you get to see him? Well, luckily, he doesn't need to see you, you don't need any magic, you just need the Tools in this book to fix yourself. He taught me all about the Monkey, but he also shared a number of his other ideas and Tools with me, then put them on to an mp3 that has been absolutely brilliant to listen to.

In one afternoon and with that mp3, he taught me enough that I was able to go back to work within days. I could see light at the end of the tunnel and, most importantly, I had learned a totally new way of thinking. I now realized that all of the things that I had worried about were not important or worrying about them served no purpose.

I learned that most of what we worry about will never happen. If it is going to happen, then worrying about it won't make the slightest difference. I learned how to calm my mind. My poor brain was overloaded with adrenalin, I was in a constant fight mindset, I needed to take time to calm my head, I needed my body to produce the calming chemicals that help combat all the adrenalin. That's when I learned so much about my inner Monkey. The Monkey on my shoulder and his constant chatter. It's the Monkey that fills your brain with self-doubt, the 'what ifs'. I needed to shut my Monkey up. How could I relax with it disastrophizing constantly?

So you don't need magic – you just need to listen to the Monkey Whisperer and then learn how to be a Monkey Tamer yourself.

Case Study 3

The Anxiety Buster
Annabel – A Monkey Called Vince

Annabel is a very elegant, stylish lady with great poise and wonderful posture. Hardly surprising, really, given she is a competitive dancer! She also is very articulate, with an excellent sense of humour. When I introduced her to her Monkey, she decided to call it Vince.

Annabel had competed in a variety of sports for many years, so it was no surprise to find that Vince was incredibly demanding, putting Annabel under lots of pressure and scrutiny. However, when you read Annabel's truly inspiring story, it becomes clear and obvious that poor old Vince the Monkey had plenty to worry about.

Annabel and I worked through most of the menu of Tools: initially, Mind the Monkey was deployed, and subsequently the Kaizen became particularly effective as she could literally take 'dancers' steps' on her journey to recovery. These days, Annabel is a fully paid-up member of the Anxiety Busters because the main Tool she used was the personal mp3. She described the recording as 'giving her the foundation and confidence to deal with all the batshit stuff that Vince was constantly chucking at me'! She once said to me that 'When dancing, the ultimate is to become the music.' She certainly achieved that goal – in life and on the dance floor . . . The dancer had finally become the dance.

I heard about Don through a serendipitous meeting with a client of his who was out shopping with his fiancée prior to an appointment. Somehow we all got talking. Two years later I found myself in Don's warm and inviting studio at his home in Bath because I wanted to change my life.

A tall order, or so I supposed.

I could never get beyond the endless negative script in my brain. I have been involved in competitive sport throughout my life but had never persevered enough to fulfil any kind of potential. It wasn't until I stopped competing in sport that I decided to give dancing a go.

As is typical of me, I threw myself into it and started dating my dance teacher. Soon I was dancing every day. However, I knew deep down that something wasn't right. I was always nervous before and during a lesson, and put it down to my perfectionist tendencies. I realize through working with Don that the nerves were my Monkey – Vince – protesting. Why? I'll come back to that later.

I discussed entering competitions with my teacher and now boyfriend, but it became clear to me that he didn't want to compete. I was unsure myself, because if I got as nervous as I did in my lessons, how would I ever control my anxiety in a competitive situation? I was very conflicted and had so many inner voices that I had a hard time knowing which one was mine.

I told Don something about my background. That I had been adopted into a strict, conservative middle-class family when I was a baby. My father, in fact, was a mini-dictator and my dear mother just complied. Throughout my childhood I was tormented by my adoptive brother, and I feel now that my need for acceptance is why I wanted to win at everything so badly. I understood later that my Monkey, Vince, was trying to save me from being disappointed, judged and rejected, so whenever things got hard I just gave in.

My teacher/boyfriend, I was to discover, had his own issues. One of which was blowing hot and cold during my lessons. I was either destined for dancing greatness or made to feel discouraged and inept. On one occasion I started to punch my own face during a lesson (I know, I know!), and even managed to break a chair on the studio floor. Another time, I had been forced into a step by my teacher/boyfriend whilst partnering him during a class, and was humiliated when I pushed back. Once, I was whistled at when he wanted to get my attention – all in good humour, apparently. All of this went on over quite a long period of time, and there was good stuff in between, and so . . . and so . . .

Fast-forward a little, a few months after I had my first meeting with Don, I became seriously ill. I spent ten days in hospital and had time to really listen to my internal chatter and reflect . . . I concluded Vince was over-protective, but he wasn't wrong about my dance teacher. I resolved, from my hospital bed, to change my life. First, I needed to start driving on motorways again. Second, I needed to dump my dance teacher/boyfriend. Third, I needed to find a new teacher with whom I wouldn't get romantically involved! Fourth, I was going to start competing.

As I write, I am looking at a little trophy on my shelf, which I won recently in a teacher/student dance competition. I have competed across England and abroad. I have made many new friends through dancing, and whilst the winning is nice, of course, I always feel that bit taller for having tried.

Vince and I now have a cooperative relationship, not a co-dependent one. We – that is, Vince and I – achieved all the above together a full year after my illness. I won't lie, we were really scared. But we were prepared, and when the music started . . . some magic happened.

I just started dancing.

Part III

Worrier to Warrior

Accidental Mind Coaches

So now you have a package of ten Tools to help you manage your Monkey Mind and change your life for the better in so many ways. You are all set to become your own mind coach, make your own decisions, and look forward to a future where you are calm, relaxed and confident. A future where anxiety is always under control, where you sleep and eat well, enjoy life and, day by day, become the best version of yourself.

However, before you waltz off into this beautiful life ahead of you, a quick final word of warning: be on the look-out for Accidental Mind Coaches (AMCs)! Let me explain . . .

I often wonder how much potential is lost, how many dreams shattered, and even how much health is ruined by AMCs? Today's fast-moving world is overflowing with people offering advice, commenting, criticizing and analysing – often without being asked to do so. It is hard enough to maintain a good level of confidence without an assorted posse of people offering their opinions, whether someone

217

has asked for them or not. To be fair, some of these 'advisers' are well meaning; others, however, are definitely not! Both types can cause significant negative mental consequences for others.

So, what exactly is an AMC? Let me give you a few examples. A racing driver I was working with told me that once, when he was on the grid, sitting in his car just before the start of a race, a senior member of his team reached into the cockpit, shook his hand and offered the following bit of advice: 'Don't crash, mate!' This was possibly meant as a jovial sign-off, but it is actually a classic case of Accidental Mind Coaching.

The reality is that when someone makes this kind of comment at any time of danger, excitement or emotion, it is likely to bypass your conscious mind 'filter' and go *straight* to your subconscious. In this particular instance, the crucial word is obviously 'crash' and, for the poor racing driver, it became incredibly difficult to stop an alarming image of a crash from swirling in his head – not really what you need seconds before starting a 200-mph race!

A world-famous golfer I know was playing a big tournament one season when he came up to a very short but challenging par-3 hole, with the green marooned on the other side of a small lake. As he prepared to take his shot, his 'supportive' father in the crowd shouted, half-jokingly, 'Don't put it in the water, son!' Guess what happened next . . .

It's not just world-famous sports stars who suffer from AMC damage. My wife, Jane, is hopeless at tennis – or so she says. In fact, she is certain of this, because she firmly believes she has 'no hand–eye coordination'. This inner doubt started at school when a (hopefully) well-meaning teacher excused a poorly executed backhand by blaming it on Jane's poor hand–eye coordination. Her schoolmates, tennis partners and coaches continued the theme. I can clearly remember both her parents telling me she was hopeless at tennis . . . because 'everybody said so'!

She had been 'accidentally hypnotized' and programmed for ever to believe she is rubbish at tennis. In fact, my wife has excellent coordination skills – witness the Christmas meal for fifteen people, juggling the kitchen duties, drinks, presents, everything, all with absolute precision. Likewise, her driving is excellent. Again, a demonstration of great hand–eye coordination, and it would be nonsense to suggest otherwise, but this is what the AMCs have been doing to her since she was a little girl.

By contrast, I was pretty lucky as a lad because my AMCs were almost all positive, and the supportive words of my parents and close family were mostly helpful. I was particularly fortunate to be born into the family I was, and lucky to be taught things by them that I believe are still so valuable today. Sadly, my experience probably puts me in a minority, because I hear of so many children – young clients or just in my daily life – who are clearly being exposed to insidious and damaging influences on a daily basis.

The dangers of AMCs are present for all of us. Examples of other AMCs might include parents, grandparents, friends, coaches, teachers, lawyers, doctors, hairdressers, pub land-lords, politicians, pop stars, vicars, wives, the media, London cabbies . . . The potential to be affected by AMCs is all around us.

How many teens have been practically hypnotized into believing they are never going to make it? How many have been sabotaged by AMCs on their journeys, and dragged back into the Worry Zone?

Specifically, social media can be a highly toxic Accidental Mind Coach. The worlds of Twitter, Instagram, YouTube and other platforms are, by definition, the almost com-pletely unmoderated Wild West of personal opinion. Users post photos of themselves with a few words underneath and, hey presto, opinions quickly come flooding in. And those opinions are not, of course, all positive, which can be extremely unhelpful and, in the worst cases, downright dangerous.

Although teens are susceptible to influence – because their brains are not yet fully developed and peer pressure can be an especially powerful force in their young lives – the fact is that the same applies to anyone using social media. Fragile minds that take criticism to heart are in grave dan-ger when they use these digital platforms. Stories of social media-fuelled self-harm are a tragic reminder of the need to protect our children and, at times, ourselves from AMCs. Not wanting to sound overly alarmist, but it can sometimes be a matter of life or death.

So, how do you protect yourself from Accidental Mind

Coaches? Unfortunately, avoiding them altogether can be incredibly difficult or downright impossible, but there is some action you can take to minimize damage. The tools you have at your disposal are split into two groups: proactive and reactive.

Proactive Tools to Protect Against AMCs

1. Identify the AMCs you come into contact with regularly. Make a list if you have to, but be sure to keep this private. Have a clear idea in your mind of the individuals you need to put up a guard against to prevent them from drowning you in a sea of negativity.

2. Sit down and take some time to be more selective with your social media accounts. If you follow someone who seems to live a 'perfect' life and who posts photographic evidence of how they are so much better than everyone else on a daily basis, then what is the benefit of following them? If someone makes negative comments on your posts, you should block them. You need to take action to ringfence yourself from the dangers of damaging opinions and take precautions to protect yourself.

    If you have children who use social media – which, in reality, will be almost anyone born in the twenty-first century – then work with them to help them become aware of the dangers of AMCs online. Don't be overwhelmed by the task – I know many parents who feel it is challenging enough to get through a day of guiding, teaching and caring for children without diving into the complex and, at times, confusing world of social media. This is perfectly understandable and entirely reasonable.

That said, you wouldn't send a fourteen-year-old into a city centre and allow them to talk to strangers and take advice from anyone they happen to encounter. So why should allowing them to interact on social media without advising and guiding them beforehand be any different? In reality, it isn't easy to police this without feeling like a snoop or potentially causing family tensions. However, you can and *should* explain the dangers of populating the online world and talk about the risks of listening to AMCs. It is a very real and serious danger to the mental wellbeing of our children, but is also an area where, with a modest amount of effort and some gentle, supportive communication, you can make a *massive* difference to their mental health. (In the interests of fairness, social media can – and does – have wide-reaching, beneficial effects, such as greater social connectivity, positive role models and the provision of a global network for developing new ideas.)

3. Sit down and think about how you can engage more with people who bring positive energy into your life instead of those who are sapping yours. To avoid negative influences, you can, for example, always change the television channel (or turn it off completely), switch radio stations, block the Facebook 'friend' who clearly isn't a friend and unfollow 'twits' on Twitter.

Reactive Remedies Against AMCs

So, having identified repeat offenders, and re-framed your social circle and online activity to filter out life's waves of AMCs, what should you do if one of these pesky individuals gets through the defences and detonates one of their verbal grenades? It is true that you cannot control the majority of outside distractions, but *you can control how you react to them*. If you let AMCs sabotage your finely honed skills, then you are leaving yourself far more vulnerable to making errors and not fulfilling or maximizing your potential.

So, how should you react to these unwanted advisers if they somehow get through with their toxic opinions?

1. Tell yourself to act as if you are protected by an invisible bubble or forcefield, one so strong that all negativity – whatever its source – simply bounces off it, leaving you completely unharmed. You can work hard at visualizing this. Really get into the detail – you

could even hear an imaginary *ping* as the negativity of the AMC is deflected and disintegrates into harmless debris.

2. If the AMC's words have already had an impact on you, remove the unwanted thoughts and feelings: deliberately and immediately replace any negative suggestions with opposing, positive opposites (see Tool 2: Mind the Monkey! – page 51).

3. Use slow Zen Breaths to remain calm (see Tool 1 – page 31).

4. URGENTLY create a 'can-do' Hollywood Movie script in your mind (see Tool 4 – page 87). You do not have to star in somebody else's movie of doom and gloom. Instead, you can write, direct, produce and be the star of your own Hollywood blockbuster.

5. Use the Kaizen Tool (see Tool 3 – page 71) to find something challenging to do every day – no matter how small – to boost your confidence so you will become more Warrior-like when AMC flak is incoming.

6. Be absolutely clear with yourself that whatever the AMC has told you you can't do, simply put on your Warrior armour and *just do it anyway.*

Using these Tools – either to prevent AMCs impacting you in the first place or to minimize any damage if they do somehow sneak through – will enable you to break free from their restrictive and destructive 'advice'. Always remain vigilant, though – raise your antennae and increase the sensitivity of your radar so you know when AMCs are on the prowl, and relax in the knowledge that you now have the Tools at hand to deal with them.

Before You Go . . .

I have absolutely loved writing this book for you. As that process comes to an end, your adventure continues – and remember, enjoying the journey is the best part! So far, you have been reading this book and listening to my words of advice, just as my clients do when they visit my home for a session. However, the next 'chapter' is super-exciting: you are now armed with a detailed understanding of how your Monkey Mind works and your OWN mental Tool Box, which means you have all the techniques and ideas to transform your life permanently – by BEING YOUR OWN MIND COACH.

You now know how to enjoy wonderfully replenishing breathing; you are aware of the importance of being able to Mind the Monkey; you can take small steps to make big differences; you can star in your own Hollywood Movie and turbo-charge your confidence; you are equipped to slow down your life, give your brain a workout, and even boost your immune system. To top it all, you can end each day with a restful, recharging night of fantastic-quality sleep. With these Tools in your possession, you should be well qualified to keep anxiety, stress, depression, and any of the other hurdles we all face, at bay.

Some of these Tools can be used in a proactive way so that you remain calm, relaxed and confident. (As JFK said, 'The time to repair the roof is when the sun is shining.') Other Tools will enable you to react quickly when you need to reconnect your mind with your body, regain control from the Monkey and restore some balance in your life, whatever the challenge. Combined, these Tools will give you the confidence that, no matter what life throws at you, there are techniques and ideas you can follow to make it through and bounce back better than ever!

I have one final 'bonus' for you, and it is possibly the most rewarding aspect of my job: once you become adept at using these Tools yourself, and start to enjoy the real, tangible benefits, you will want to share these ideas with your nearest and dearest. You might see a friend taking too much advice from someone who you now know is a damaging Accidental Mind Coach; maybe you will think of a Tool that will help a family member overcome an unexpected bump in the road; or perhaps a teenager you know needs to hear all about their Monkey, give it a name and start to regain control from it. By using the brain-tuning Tools in this book, not only can you learn how to be your own Mind Coach, but you can also teach your kids, family and friends, and by doing so you will help people to move progressively and gently, at their own pace, from Worrier to Warrior.

If I could have my dad back here with me for a few moments, I would like to think that he would be proud of me for helping the clients who walk through my door, through using the Tools I have shared in this book. Maybe he would even have smiled, in that particularly Northern way that expresses unspoken pride. I certainly know that he would be even more proud of the fact that, once you understand and put into practice the ideas in this book, you can share them far and wide. Just as he spread his expertise and energy all around the Hattersley estate in Manchester, so too can you, by studying these ideas, mastering them and then sharing them with people you want to help. Is there any better way to improve your own life than by helping others?

So, we have now arrived at the moment when you leave me and walk off into your own, bright future. Off you go – I've talked the talk, now walk your walk. No hurries, no worries. Just float with life's challenges when they come to you, as they surely will. Only now, everything will be different when it comes to how you react, how you deal with life's ups and downs, and how you move forward.

Remember that life is a dance, not a wrestling match. So, slow down, remember that YOU ARE THE BOSS, and always make sure you are kind to yourself.

After my dad died, I found a newspaper article in his personal effects. It contained an interview he'd done for the *Manchester Evening News*. As a hobby, my dad used to fly a small plane and so this particular article called him 'the Flying Doctor'. As I sat there reading this article, I was astonished to discover how he sometimes used to parachute jump – I never knew that! The journalist asked him why on earth he would want to do such a thing and my father replied, 'Because every time I parachute out of a plane and land safely, nothing bothers me for weeks and weeks.'

In so many ways, that anecdote mirrors where you are now . . . There is a whole new world to explore out there – one of excitement, enjoyment, reward and achievement, and you are now fully qualified to experience all the wonders that this life has to offer, safe in the knowledge that your newfound expertise and confidence will act as your parachute to support you and keep you safe. All you have to do is make the first move.

So, go on . . . What are you waiting for? Make the leap into the brilliant sunshine and your amazing future. It's fantastic out there . . . Have fun!

And don't believe everything you think – or what the Monkey tells you.

What Elite Sports Stars Say About Don Macpherson

George Ford, England Rugby star

'One area people don't invest enough time in these days is the mental side. Everybody trains physically, on the field or in the gym. But the mental side is such a huge part. Don's been brilliant . . . he gives you tools to go away and use, to ensure you're training your brain.'

Anthony Watson, England Rugby star

'The effect it has had on my game and my ability to control nerves and to remain calm has been huge. I can't thank him enough for the work he has done for me.'

Damon Hill, 1996 Formula One world champion

'I first met Don when I was still racing, about 1997, and we talked a lot about the mind in a sporting context. Naturally, this was an area of special interest to me and I quickly realized that he knew what he was talking about. What we learn in sport about our mind is a very transferable skill to all areas of life, and I'm keen to see what Don has to say on how we help young people counter the onslaught of our contemporary Western culture.'

Pat Cash, 1987 Wimbledon champion

'I decided to try some mind management to help me deal with pressure, expectations, injuries and the uncertainty that follows many an athlete at the end of their career. I found Don's work truly beneficial and his knowledge of the pro sportsperson's mind impressive, to say the least. Don has the ability to understand and navigate what can be a minefield of distractions and issues.'

Coco Vandeweghe, US Grand Slam Doubles winner and twice Grand Slam Singles semi-finalist

'Don Macpherson: the monkey whisperer, the monkey tamer, the man that loves Jaguar cars . . . I like to call Don the man that proved me wrong, and I don't say that often. My first chat with Don involved him giving me a run-down about who he is and what he does. All that mumbo-jumbo can sound very fascinating to most people, but in my no-nonsense American fashion I said, 'That's cool and all, but I don't think you mental-coach guys are worth anything – so prove me wrong.' Well, here I am eating my words. Every mp3, Skype, and even a trip to Bath, England was worth it. I am now a calmer, cooler 'Coco Cat'! In taming my monkey mind, Don has brought me to heights that I didn't think I would ever reach, not only in tennis but in life. Lovely jubbly stuff (as Don would say).'

Alexander Rossi, American IndyCar Racer and winner of the Indy 500

'Choosing to work with Don was one of the best decisions that I made off-track in my racing career. Motorsport is as much a mental game as it is a sport of physicality and bravery and many drivers struggle to overcome the mental barriers that go along with the immense pressure of competing against a clock, as well as other teams and drivers. Don provided me with the tools to be able to compartmentalize all of these pressures so that, when I was behind the wheel, I could focus solely on performing at my best and extracting the most performance out of the machine. With his help I was able to become one with the present and visualize the results and success that I wanted so badly to achieve. His practices of achieving mental clarity have stayed with me every time that I have stepped into a race car for the past five years, as well as on a daily basis in my normal life. I can truly say that I wouldn't be where I am today without his help.'

Kazuki Nakajima, Formula One Driver and three-time 24 Hours of Le Mans winner

'I started to work with Don when I was racing for the Williams F1 team. At the time I had to deal with so many new challenges all at the same time, including huge pressure to perform on the race track. The work with Don certainly helped me to deal with the 'monkey' in my brain and to focus what I had to do in a racing car. All those sessions to practise meditation, breathing, visualization, are still clearly in my mind and these are my assets even now. I believe these techniques are useful not only in extreme conditions but also on a daily basis . . . I hope this book will find many people who need help!'

David Brabham, 2009 24 Hours of Le Mans winner and Formula One racing driver

'I had an experience in 1987 where I got into a mental state that took my performance in a car to a level I never knew existed. It was the start of a journey of discovery into how the mind plays a huge role in creating our reality. From that moment, I looked at how I could improve my thinking to find that extra bit behind the wheel. I feel very lucky to know Don.'

Dr Kerry Spackman, Cognitive Neuroscientist

'Quite simply, Don knows what works and what doesn't, so you can trust his advice, just as some of the world's most successful athletes have. It has been a genuine pleasure working with Don over the years.'

Mike Ford, Leicester Tigers coach and former England and Ireland Rugby Union coach

'Don understood from the get-go that I wanted a mental-skills coach who made my players better *rugby players*, not amateur psychologists. All the players loved the way Don works, making "the way the brain works" simple for them to understand . . . which is no easy task when you have forty different human beings with different ways of learning and their own way of looking at things, certainly unique to rugby. I only wish I had met Don earlier, because he gave me Tools and helped me to enjoy life more and to be a better person.'

References

Tool 8: The Immune-system Booster

Page 156: **we can, and should, influence our ANS:** Kox, M., et al., 'Voluntary Activation of the Sympathetic Nervous System and Attenuation of the Innate Immune Response in Humans', *PNAS*, 111(20) (2014), 7379–84.

Page 157: **Hof has been the subject of several scientific studies:** Muzik, O., et al., 'Brain Over Body – A Study on the Willful Regulation of Autonomic Function During Cold Exposure', *NeuroImage*, 172 (2018).

Acknowledgements

Firstly, a big thanks to all of you who took the time to read my book. I really do hope you liked it, and that you were able to take something from it that will help you be more calm, relaxed and confident . . . to be your own Mind Coach and Brain Tuner.

My biggest thank you is to my wife, Jane, who trusted me and allowed me to 'do my thing' while she took care of absolutely everything else. Quite simply, without Jane this book would never have been written, because there wouldn't have been anything to write about. Thank you, Jane, for everything . . .

Thanks to my lovely daughters Katie and Hannah . . . for simply being Katie and Hannah. I am very proud of the stylish, witty, caring young ladies you have become.

If I could now say to my dad that I have 'finally finished a book', he would probably assume that I'd actually managed to 'read a book', certainly not write one! So, big thanks to Michelle Signore and all her talented and creative team at Transworld Publishers for making it happen, and to Martin

Acknowledgements

Roach for all your mentoring, wit, wisdom, and inexhaustible patience. Thank you to Natalie Jerome for spotting that 'Monkey Whispering' could also translate into a book, and your introduction to the professional people I needed at the right time and place.

I must also give huge thanks to my friend and tennis partner Peter 'G' who, thirty-one years ago, just when I most needed some direction, gave me a 'nudge' which, beyond doubt, started my long and exciting journey to becoming a mind coach. Thank you, P.G.!

Last, but by no means least, thank you to all of you who came to me for some Mind Coaching for whatever reason, sporty or otherwise, and allowed me to play a small part in your journey – it was my privilege and I am sure I learned as much, if not more, from you than you did from me!

A Note on Your Personal Mp3

Use this link to listen to your own personal 'Anxiety Buster' mp3. It contains guided relaxation and visualization, specifically designed to reduce anxiety levels, so that you can feel – and be – more calm, relaxed and confident. Please listen where you can safely close your eyes and hopefully won't be disturbed for the duration of the mp3. Hope you enjoy it!

https://www.donmacpherson.co.uk/bonusbookcontent

Password: Bookcode2

Audio engineered by Jonathan Garside
Music composed by Christopher Lloyd Clarke
Vocals by Don Macpherson

About the Author

Don Macpherson is a British mind coach who combines mind-management techniques and hypnosis with an in-depth knowledge of modern neuroscience. His most high-profile work has been coaching dozens of world-class sports professionals, including F1 racing drivers, Premiership footballers, international rugby players and Wimbledon tennis champions. Over thirty years Don has also helped countless other people with a diverse range of issues such as anxiety, stress, lack of confidence and relationship problems. Don takes challenging mind-management concepts, and makes them easy to understand and to put into practice.